WJEC GCSE

ENGLISH

 **ROGER LANE**

ENGLISH
ENGLISH LANGUAGE
ENGLISH LITERATURE

WJEC CBAC

OXFORD
UNIVERSITY PRESS

OXFORD
UNIVERSITY PRESS

Great Clarendon Street, Oxford OX2 6DP

Oxford University Press is a department of the University of Oxford.
It furthers the University's objective of excellence in research,
scholarship, and education by publishing worldwide in

Oxford   New York

Auckland   Cape Town   Dar es Salaam   Hong Kong   Karachi
Kuala Lumpur   Madrid   Melbourne   Mexico City   Nairobi
New Delhi   Shanghai   Taipei   Toronto

With offices in

Argentina   Austria   Brazil   Chile   Czech Republic   France   Greece
Guatemala   Hungary   Italy   Japan   Poland   Portugal   Singapore
South Korea   Switzerland   Thailand   Turkey   Ukraine   Vietnam

Oxford is a registered trade mark of Oxford University Press
in the UK and in certain other countries

Database right Oxford University Press (maker)

First published 2010

Third party website addresses referred to in this publication are
provided by Oxford University Press in good faith and for
information only and Oxford University Press disclaims any
responsibility for the material contained therein

British Library Cataloguing in Publication Data

Data available

ISBN 978-0-19-831082-2

10 9 8 7 6 5 4 3 2 1

Printed in Spain by Cayfosa-Impresia Ibérica

CONTENTS

INTRODUCTION

How to use this book if you are studying…

SECTION 1: READING

SECTION 2: WRITING

SECTION 3 SPEAKING and LISTENING

How to use this book if you're studying

ENGLISH

There is a great deal of crossover between the GCSE English specification and the English Language and English Literature specifications. However, it's easy to find exactly what you need for the spec you are following. Wherever you see this symbol, you will find information specific to the English specification.

The WJEC GCSE English specification consists of four units.

Unit 1: English in the Daily World (Reading)			
	Assessment	Weighting	AOs covered
READING Answer structured questions on two non-fiction texts.	Written paper 1 hour	20% 40 marks	AO3

Non-Fiction Texts are covered in **Chapter 1.1** of this book. You will learn skills in close reading and how to compare a variety of non-fiction texts. You will also have the opportunity to practise your skills with exam-style questions and to see excerpts from sample student answers.

Unit 2: English in the Daily World (Writing)			
	Assessment	Weighting	AOs covered
WRITING Complete two tasks on transactional writing.	Written paper 1 hour	20% 40 marks	AO3

Information and Ideas are covered in **Chapter 2.2**. You will learn about the different types of text, and how you should go about composing your own text. You will also have the chance to improve your accuracy in spelling and grammar.

Unit 3: English in the World of the Imagination Section A: Literary Texts

	Assessment	Weighting	AOs covered
READING Write one assignment on a Shakespeare play linked to a range of thematically linked literary heritage poetry from the WJEC collection, and one assignment studying a Different Cultures prose text.	Controlled Assessment	20% 40 marks	AO2

Chapter 1.3 is dedicated to the links between contemporary poetry and Shakespeare, and you will find examples of Controlled Assessment tasks and sample answers included there. For your study of a Different Cultures prose text, you will find full support and excerpts from all of the prescribed texts in **Chapter 1.4**.

Unit 3: English in the World of the Imagination Section B: Open Writing

	Assessment	Weighting	AOs covered
WRITING Write one piece of first-person and one piece of third-person narrative writing.	Controlled Assessment	20% 40 marks	AO3

Narrative writing is covered in **Chapter 2.1**, which also has examples of first- and third-person narratives and guidance on what makes a successful piece of creative writing. You will also have the opportunity to examine a number of examples of successful (and less successful!) student work to allow you to improve your own style.

Unit 4: Speaking and Listening

	Assessment	Weighting	AOs covered
SPEAKING AND LISTENING Complete three speaking and listening tasks: • an individual presentation • a group discussion • a role-play.	Controlled Assessment	10% 20 marks	AO1

All three of the tasks are covered in **Chapter 3.1**. You will find a number of examples of speaking and listening tasks, as well as examiner's tips for successful speaking and listening work.

How to use this book if you're studying
ENGLISH LANGUAGE

Although this book covers all three of the WJEC GCSE English specifications, it is easy to find just the information you need for the spec you are covering. Wherever you see this symbol , you will find information specific to the English Language specification.

The WJEC GCSE English Language specification consists of four units.

Unit 1: Studying Written Language			
	Assessment	Weighting	AOs covered
READING Answer structured questions on two non-fiction texts.	Written paper 1 hour	20% 40 marks	AO3

Non-Fiction Texts are covered in **Chapter 1.1** of this book. You will learn skills in close reading and how to compare a variety of non-fiction texts. You will also have the opportunity to practise your skills with exam-style questions and to see excerpts from sample student answers.

Unit 2: Using Written Language			
	Assessment	Weighting	AOs covered
WRITING Complete two tasks on transactional writing.	Written paper 1 hour	20% 40 marks	AO4

Information and Ideas are covered in **Chapter 2.2**. You will learn about different types of text, and how you should go about composing your own text. You will also have the chance to improve your accuracy in spelling and grammar.

Unit 3: Literary Reading and Creative Writing Section A: Studying Written Language			
	Assessment	Weighting	AOs covered
READING Write a sustained response to an extended literary text.	Controlled Assessment	15% 40 marks	AO3

For your Controlled Assessment task you can choose to study a play by Shakespeare or a text chosen from the GCSE English Literature set text lists excluding poetry. Although **Chapters 1.3, 1.4 and 1.5** are focused around the study of these texts in the GCSE English and English Literature specs, you will find useful information in them relevant to your exploration of literature, whether it is Shakespeare (Chapters 1.3 and 1.5), drama (Chapter 1.5) or prose (Chapters 1.4 and 1.5).

Unit 3: Literary Reading and Creative Writing
Section B: Using Language

	Assessment	Weighting	AOs covered
WRITING Write one piece of descriptive writing and one piece of narrative/expressive writing.	Controlled Assessment	15% 40 marks	AO4

Both narrative and descriptive writing are covered in **Chapter 2.1** (Creative Writing). You will be able to learn about the features of both types of writing and what you should try to include in your work. You will also have the opportunity to examine a number of examples of successful (and less successful!) student work to allow you to improve your own style.

Unit 4: Spoken Language
Section A: Using Language

	Assessment	Weighting	AOs covered
SPEAKING AND LISTENING Complete three speaking and listening tasks: • an individual presentation • a group discussion • a role-play.	Controlled Assessment	20% 40 marks	AO1

All three of the tasks are covered in **Chapter 3.1**. You will find a number of examples of speaking and listening tasks, as well as examiner's tips for successful speaking and listening work.

Unit 4: Spoken Language
Section B: Studying Spoken Language

	Assessment	Weighting	AOs covered
SPEAKING AND LISTENING Write an assignment on an aspect of spoken language.	Controlled Assessment	10% 20 marks	AO2

The study of spoken language is the focus of **Chapter 3.2**. This is a new area of GCSE study, but you will find all the support you need to tackle your assessment with confidence.

How to use this book if you're studying
ENGLISH LITERATURE

Much of your study of English Literature will involve getting to grips with your set texts. However, there are also a number of skills that you need to be able to apply to your literature studies, and you will find many of them within this book. Wherever you see this symbol , you will find information specific to the English Literature specification.

The WJEC GCSE English Literature specification consists of three units.

Unit 1: Prose (Different Cultures) and Poetry (Contemporary) Section A: Individual texts in context			
	Assessment	Weighting	AOs covered
Answer two questions on a chosen prose text.	Written paper 1 hour	21% 30 marks	AO1 AO2 AO4
Section B: Comparative Study			
	Assessment	Weighting	AOs covered
Compare two contemporary unseen poems.	Written paper 1 hour	14% 20 marks	AO1 AO2 AO3

Unit 1 is tested by one two-hour exam paper that is divided into two sections. You should aim to spend an hour on each section.

Section A deals with Different Cultures Prose, which is covered in **Chapter 1.4**. In this chapter, you will learn some of the features common to prose texts, and find excerpts from all of the five texts prescribed for this unit.

In Section B, you will have the opportunity to explore, respond to and compare two unseen contemporary poems. You will find all the preparation you need in **Chapter 1.2**.

Unit 2 Option A: Literary Heritage Drama and Contemporary Prose			
	Assessment	Weighting	AOs covered
Study two texts and answer two questions on each of them.	Written paper 2 hours	40% 60 marks	AO1 AO2 AO4

OR Unit 2 Option B: Contemporary Drama and Literary Heritage Prose			
	Assessment	Weighting	AOs covered
Study two texts and answer two questions on each of them.	Written paper 2 hours	40% 60 marks	AO1 AO2 AO4

Unit 2 is tested by one exam paper but there will be two options to choose from. If you choose to study Unit 2a, you will study a drama text from the English/Irish/Welsh literary heritage and a contemporary prose text. You will find support for the study of drama and prose in **Chapter 1.5**.

If you choose to study Unit 2b, you will study a contemporary drama text and a prose text from the English/Irish/Welsh literary heritage. Both drama and prose are covered in **Chapter 1.5**.

Unit 3: Poetry and Drama (Literary Heritage)			
	Assessment	Weighting	AOs covered
Write an assignment linking a play by Shakespeare and a group of thematically linked poems from the WJEC collection.	Controlled Assessment	25% 40 marks	AO1 AO2 AO3

Unit 3 is assessed by a single Controlled Assessment. **Chapter 1.3** is dedicated to the links between contemporary poetry and Shakespeare, and you will find examples of Controlled Assessment tasks and sample answers included there.

TO THE STUDENT

If you stick around to use this book properly, I hope that you will find that it communicates to you directly. English courses may become more and more complex, but English itself should always be clear and coherent. English that means nothing is worth nothing. Read for meaning, and write good sense.

With or without the help of this book, believe in yourself. Good luck!

Roger Lane

Author's Acknowledgements

Thanks to Nicola Dutton: pushing from the start line to the finish; the coach.

Thanks to Hugh Lester: for good sense all of the time and good humour most of the time; the director.

FEATURES OF THIS BOOK

This book provides a number of useful features to help you find your way through the course. Here is a quick guide to what you can expect:

- **Focus on the Exam/Controlled Assessment** – these green boxes appear at the start of each chapter and contain key details about the Exam or Controlled Assessment covered in the chapter. The colour-coded hand icons should help you to see how this information relates to the subject you are studying – whether it is English, English Language or English Literature.

- **Examiner's Tips** – these blue tip boxes appear throughout the book and contain valuable pointers on how to improve your work and how to perform to your best ability. There are also some useful tips about 'what not to do' so you should pay attention to these too!

- **Exam/Controlled Assessment Practice** – you will find this section at the end of each chapter. It provides example questions based on real exam papers or Controlled Assessment tasks.

- **Sample Student Responses and Examiner's Comments** – this book provides you with a full range of sample student answers along with feedback from a real examiner. These comments can help you to better understand what is required of you and identify ways to gain a higher mark.

- **Self-assessment Panels** – these handy checklists provide a straightforward way of assessing your progress. Answer the questions honestly and work out what you need to do next to boost your performance.

- **Functional Skills** – some sections of this book are marked with a Functional Skills logo, . This content will help you to practise using Functional Skills in writing and speaking and listening.

FOCUS ON THE EXAM   E UNIT 1   LA UNIT 1

GCSE English Language Unit 1

GCSE English Unit 1

The content and questions for this written paper on non-fiction texts will be the same in GCSE English and GCSE English Language.

This unit will test the reading of two non-fiction texts through structured questions. Non-fiction texts may include: fact-sheets, leaflets, letters, extracts from autobiographies, biographies, diaries, advertisements, reports, articles and digital and multi-modal texts of various kinds from newspapers and magazines, brochures and the internet. Visual material will always be included in the material used.

The written exam on non-fiction texts puts your independent reading skills under the spotlight. Take note of the broad range of skills required:

- **location and reorganization** – finding things and using your own words
- **inference** – reading 'between the lines'
- **appreciation of style** – looking at the way the author writes.

Close reading

When close-reading a non-fiction text, you will need to position yourself by establishing who the text is aimed at or who it is written for. This is the **audience** of the text. Then you should look at the **purpose** of the text or why it was written.

> **Look carefully at the following texts. Who are they aimed at? What are they trying to do? Identify both the audience and purpose for each example and explain your answers.**

STEER CLEAR OF CAR CRIME

A lot of vehicle crime is the result of criminals seeing opportunities and taking them. You may not suffer from car crime just because you own a car, and it is not something you should fear. You can easily outsmart most criminals by taking simple steps to secure your car.

2

Good news for you, Mr Jones!

You have been selected to enter the

Winners Galore £16,960 prize draw!

You have already come through our detailed consideration and selection stages and are now close to the prize allocation stage. All you have to do is reply to this letter to receive any prize which might **ALREADY** have been allocated to you.

Look again at examples 1 and 2. Both of them use **direct address**, meaning they talk directly to you. Direct address contributes to the tone of the text.

3

AIR CADETS

Challenge yourself – the next generation needs you

Seeking a new challenge? The Air Cadet Organization needs high calibre adult volunteers to run its activities. Flying, climbing, ghyll scrambling, shooting, bands, rugby, football and netball are just a taste of the activities offered by the Air Cadets to youngsters aged 13–20.
But to deliver this exciting programme – and our respected academic syllabus – we need volunteers from all walks of life, especially professionals.

Who or what is the target audience in example 3? What is the purpose of the text? Explain your answers.

Look at the health and well-being information below. Consider the tone of voice used by the writer of the text. Is the voice used, on the whole, informal and chatty or formal and reserved? Find some evidence to support your answer.

4

Health Challenge Wales

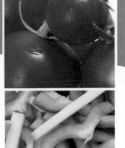

Health Challenge Wales

is about better health and well-being information and activity.

Its message to you is that small and inexpensive changes to your daily routine can make a big difference to your health.

Here's how…

❖ Everyday activities such as taking the stairs instead of the lift or walking some of the way to work can make a big difference.

❖ Eating five portions of fruit and vegetables a day could add three years to your life and quitting smoking could add five years.

So making the effort is worth it — and you feel better along the way too.

Want to find out more?

To find out more about leading a healthier lifestyle, phone 0845 604 4050 for the information to get you started. Or visit the website at www.wales.gov.uk/healthchallenge.

Now read a small part of a travel article on Namibia, in south-west Africa. As you read, consider the title or headline, the sentence types and the choice of words.

5

Namibia: Land of contrasts

Feel the spray of the cold Atlantic Ocean on your face while the desert sun warms your back. Take on the challenge of driving along rocky canyons in a seemingly barren desert, only to turn the bend and come face to face with a herd of elephants. Or float gently **down a cool river where hippos are your closest companions. At night,** lay your head on a pillow of soft sand, with a blanket of stars overhead and drift off to sleep. Or snuggle up in a bungalow and listen wide-eyed as the powerful roar of lions seems to shake the walls.

Welcome to Namibia, a stunning land of contrasts.

1. Comment on the meaning of the headline in the article about Namibia, and how it connects with the content below it.
2. The words and phrases are intended to make Namibia seem attractive. Pick out two or three that help to create a favourable mood and atmosphere.
3. Explain the effect of imperative (or command) forms of verbs throughout the short extract (for example, 'Feel the spray...', 'Take on the challenge...', 'Float gently...')

The next article advertises an attraction closer to home...

Rhondda Heritage Park Experience

A living testament to the mining communities of the world-famous Rhondda Valleys. The park offers a fascinating insight into the rich culture and character of the South Wales Valleys in a unique, entertaining and educational environment for all ages.

The sentence above is very dense. If you have to explain it in plain English, what would you say? Finish the following sentence: 'It is trying to say that the Rhondda Heritage Park...'

Look at the extracts below, thinking about the audience, purpose, format and tone. Then write two or three sentences explaining each text.

7 Come, if you dare, on a ghost tour around historic, haunted Llancaiach Fawr. Nothing is staged, so if you see or hear something unearthly – it's real!

8 **The world's most dangerous road**
Every year it is estimated 200 to 300 people die on a stretch of road less than 50 miles long. In one year alone, 25 vehicles plunged off the road and into a ravine that runs alongside.

9 How to survive a bear attack
If you see a bear, talk to the bear. Make sure he sees you. Hold your arms high above your head; this will make you look like a much bigger animal to him. Continue to talk and slowly back away. If you run he will chase you.

10 The wolf
In Britain it is over 250 years since the forests provided the last refuge for wolves trying to escape the all-out war that was waged against them.

11 World Challenge Expeditions started to organize educational expeditions a decade ago. We work with students from all walks of life, from initial planning and fundraising stages all the way through to the expeditions themselves. We don't organize travel holidays; we set challenges for young people to overcome, enjoy and learn from.

12 Treat me as a person first, then ask about my disability. There is nothing I can't achieve because I'm a wheelchair user. My personal belief is that achievement is about how much you believe in yourself, knowing what it will take to reach your goals and working very hard to get there.

13 Get out and enjoy the BIG country.
With a huge variety of landscapes, activities and places of interest, Wales is the perfect solution for those who want to experience something completely different.

Comparing texts

In your exam, you will read two non-fiction texts, so you will need to practise using your close reading skills to compare two related texts.

The following texts provide two views of a seaside resort. The audience and purpose of each text is different. Try to identify them.

14
No childhood is quite complete without remembered dreams of halcyon days spent at the seaside paddling in the waters or playing on the sands.
Its popularity has stood the test of time. The traditional still thrives in the form of Punch and Judy shows, donkey rides and organized games.
The Promenade itself is a hive of activity during the glorious months of summer. For fun and frivolity, sunbathing and people-watching, Llandudno is truly the place where memories are made.

15
To my consternation, the town was packed with weekending pensioners. Coaches from all over were parked along the side streets. Every hotel I called at was full and in every dining room I could see crowds of nodding heads spooning soup and conversing happily.
In the morning, I emerged from the guesthouse into a world drained of colour. The sky was low and heavy and the sea vast, lifeless and grey. As I walked along, rain began to fall.

In what ways are the images of Llandudno in the two texts different? Express these differences in clear, controlled sentences.

Now look at these two texts about a serious issue with polarized views.

16 Thousands of whales and dolphins are killed each year – drowned by unscrupulous fishermen whose only concern is the profit from their next catch.

17

Whaling in the Faroe Islands

The Faroese have been catching whales for a thousand years. Since 1990, the annual catch of whales has averaged about 1,000. Recent estimates put the numbers of North Atlantic whales at 778,000, so their future can never be threatened by whale hunts in the Faroes.

Explain the attitudes of each writer in the texts above. Use evidence from the texts. Don't try to do this in one sentence.

The chef Jamie Oliver also provokes different opinions.

Why we all hate Jamie Oliver

by Mecca Ibrahim

WHO IS JAMIE OLIVER? Well, if you live in the States there's a fair chance you haven't heard of him. If you live in the UK and you have a TV, come on... Do you switch it on occasionally? If so, you will see this mockney 'chef' appearing on countless adverts for Sainsbury's supermarket and you'll see him as the 'Naked Chef'.

Jamie has this great ability to cause emotions in people. Love him or hate him. You can't really be indifferent to him. My husband liked his first TV series. I really liked his second TV series. By the third series we both wanted to hurl the trusty food mixer at the TV.

cookingtime.blogspot

http://cookingtime.blogspot   Google

cookingtime.blogspot   YouTube

How Jamie Saved Me

The Naked Chef taught 15 jobless teenagers how to run a restaurant. Oliver has gambled £1.3 million of his own money to make the scheme a success, and the programme showed all the qualities that make the chef admirable: he is hard-working, loyal, responsible, generous and sympathetic, but even these qualities did not guarantee success.

Viewers watched in incredulity as the students appeared to rebel against 27-year-old Oliver's attempts to cajole them into working, opting instead to accuse him of using them to forward his own career and often not turning up for work at all.

What impressions of Jamie Oliver do you get from these two extracts?
Refer to to both texts to support your answer.

Exam Practice 1

Source text A

S.O.S. Save our Stanley

Accrington Stanley is a historic football club that has faced a financial struggle more than once in its history. In the 1960s the club went out of business, but the people of Accrington in Lancashire re-formed it and built it up slowly over 40 years to its former place in the Football League. Now it is facing another struggle to stay alive. Accrington is about 30 miles from Manchester and the football club is a key part of its identity.

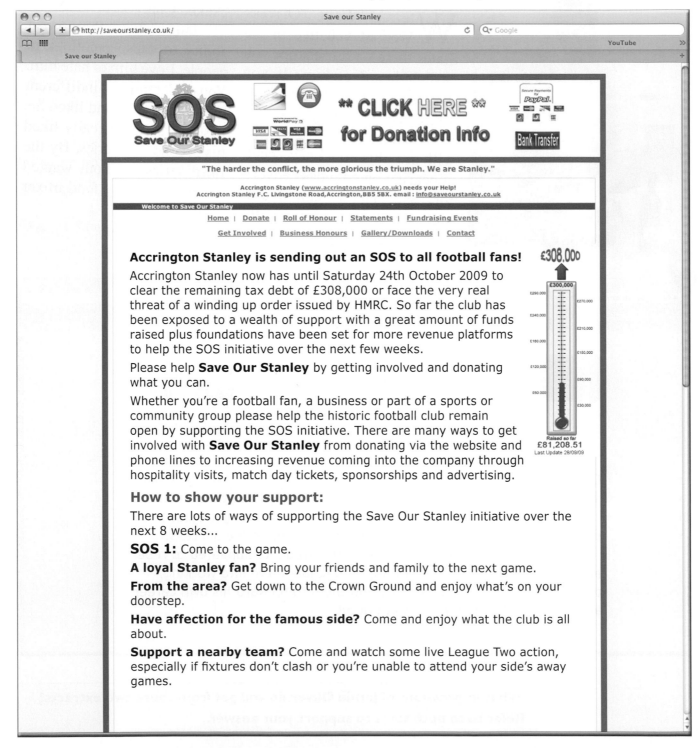

Save our Stanley

http://saveourstanley.co.uk/

SOS Save Our Stanley

** CLICK HERE **
for Donation Info

Secure Payments by PayPal

Bank Transfer

"The harder the conflict, the more glorious the triumph. We are Stanley."

Accrington Stanley (www.accringtonstanley.co.uk) needs your Help!
Accrington Stanley F.C. Livingstone Road, Accrington, BB5 5BX. email : info@saveourstanley.co.uk

Welcome to Save Our Stanley

Home | Donate | Roll of Honour | Statements | Fundraising Events
Get Involved | Business Honours | Gallery/Downloads | Contact

Accrington Stanley is sending out an SOS to all football fans!

Accrington Stanley now has until Saturday 24th October 2009 to clear the remaining tax debt of £308,000 or face the very real threat of a winding up order issued by HMRC. So far the club has been exposed to a wealth of support with a great amount of funds raised plus foundations have been set for more revenue platforms to help the SOS initiative over the next few weeks.

Please help **Save Our Stanley** by getting involved and donating what you can.

Whether you're a football fan, a business or part of a sports or community group please help the historic football club remain open by supporting the SOS initiative. There are many ways to get involved with **Save Our Stanley** from donating via the website and phone lines to increasing revenue coming into the company through hospitality visits, match day tickets, sponsorships and advertising.

£308,000

£300,000

£290,000
£270,000
£240,000
£210,000
£180,000
£150,000
£120,000
£90,000
£60,000
£30,000

Raised so far
£81,208.51
Last Update 28/09/09

How to show your support:

There are lots of ways of supporting the Save Our Stanley initiative over the next 8 weeks...

SOS 1: Come to the game.

A loyal Stanley fan? Bring your friends and family to the next game.

From the area? Get down to the Crown Ground and enjoy what's on your doorstep.

Have affection for the famous side? Come and enjoy what the club is all about.

Support a nearby team? Come and watch some live League Two action, especially if fixtures don't clash or you're unable to attend your side's away games.

> **Next Fixture at the Crown Ground:**
> **Tuesday 6th October: 7.45pm**
> Accrington Stanley vs Shrewsbury Town
> Support Save Our Stanley Initiative by purchasing tickets in advance.

SOS 2: Purchase Merchandise

Accrington Stanley is a famous brand recognised around the globe. Visit the online store that has a range of products from replica home and away shirts to scarves, key rings and car accessories and much more. **CLICK HERE** to visit Accrington Stanley's online store or come to the Crown Ground and call in the Stanley Store.

SOS 3: Donate

Credit/Debit Card, Cheque, Postal Order, Text, Phone, Paypal, Bank Transfer

For donation info **CLICK HERE**

SOS 4: Get Involved

The SOS Team are currently creating and confirming a fundraising calendar. Keep a look out on this website for the different fundraising events taking place over the next few weeks. Once each activity has been confirmed it will be posted on **SaveOurStanley.co.uk**.

Thank you for all the sponsorship and fundraising activities that are taking place across the region and, in fact, the country! To help you along the way, **CLICK HERE** to download an SOS Sponsorship form.

Hannah raids her piggy bank to help save Accrington Stanley

Clitheroe schoolgirl Hannah Holland has emptied her piggybank to help save an East Lancashire football club. The nine-year-old Pendle Primary School pupil donated just over £8 to Accrington Stanley's SOS appeal.

Wearing a t-shirt with the words "I emptied my piggy bank to save Stanley, what will YOU do?" she presented the money before the game. Hannah then watched the match from the directors' seats, and saw her side win 2-1.

Her mum Katie said: "It is an amazing feeling to have a child wanting to save Accrington Stanley without a second thought, willing to give her pocket money up to help the SOS fund."

Save our Stanley

Source text B

Manchester City are making a mockery of the game
Manchester City is a Premier League football club that has very rich owners. They are able to offer huge fees to other clubs to buy their best players, and they pay very high wages too.

Manchester City are making a mockery of the game

Carlos Tevez

Manchester City might be able to buy any footballer on the planet – but their wild excess in the transfer market won't buy them any friends or win them any respect.

Employers are all having to scale right back and making savage cuts – just like many football clubs who will next season be operating on massively reduced budgets and smaller first-team squads, while still demanding that teams deliver results.

Yet the money-bags Premier League clubs continue to prove they are completely out of step with the rest of us with their greed-is-good mentality and no-holds-barred approach to battering each other into submission with their wallets.

While many fans struggle to rake together enough cash to be able to afford tickets to watch their favourite players, doesn't it stick in the throat when you read that Manchester City's new signing Carlos Tevez will earn a staggering £39 million in wages over the next five years?

No amount of talent, goals or ability to excite fans can possibly justify anyone earning such an obscene amount of money which could feed and clothe thousands of the world's most needy.

If ever we needed proof that the football transfer market had lost touch with reality it came when Manchester City shelled out a mind-boggling £25 million fee for the Argentina star, soon to be followed by Emmanuel Adebayor for an identical fee.

Their arrival at Eastlands has sent City's spending rocketing through the £200 million barrier since Hughes took over a year ago, with the billions of owner Sheikh Mansour making his every transfer wish possible.

We may have become all too familiar with football's stinking rich throwing their money around but that does not mean to say that we've grown to accept it as the norm. The more they spend, the greedier they become and it damns them.

With mega-rich City willing to spend whatever it takes to sign the players they want, the whole game is just spiralling out of control because an extra zero is now automatically being placed on the end of every player's fee.

The crazy transfer fees currently being paid give fans unrealistic expectations and puts pressure on clubs to spend beyond their means at a time when they should be tightening their belts, which is threatening their very existence.

Only foolhardy clubs will spend for the sake of it during football's current mid-summer madness and the wise ones will wait until they can get some value for their money.

This is not the most difficult question, but you need to organize an answer by selecting distinct points and perhaps grouping them together. It is not quite a 'List...' question, but if you accumulate as many points as possible, you will be on the right lines.

Answer **all** *the following questions.*

Look at the 'S.O.S. Save Our Stanley' webpages.

1. What can people do to help Accrington Stanley Football Club in their current difficulties, according to the website?   [10]
2. How does the Save Our Stanley campaign appeal to a range of people to help Accrington Stanley Football Club?   [10]

Think about:
- what is said;
- how it is said and presented;
- the effect of the design and layout.

Now look at the newspaper article 'Manchester City are making a mockery of the game'.

3. What is the writer's attitude to the money being spent by Manchester City Football Club?   [10]

To answer the next question you will need to look at both texts.

4. The images of Manchester City Football Club and Accrington Stanley Football Club in these texts are very different. In what ways are they different?   [10]

   Refer to details in both texts to support your answer.

You definitely need to move beyond Question 1 here, and look at the 'how' (the methods of appeal) and 'the range' (different kinds of people).

Get a good, clear starting position here, because, after all, it is not too difficult to see that the writer is unimpressed by Manchester City's spending. Earn the marks with some clear selections and explanations.

A crisp, clear opening is vital. As with all comparison questions, organization is important. Don't get into a long discussion. Make the obvious point first.

Sample answers

Here are a series of sample student answers with comments from the examiner.

Student response Question 1

Donate and raise money. The club need £308,000 to pay off their tax bill so they are asking people to help them. On the website they give lots of ways fans and others can help raise money. They ask people to come to the games and bring friends along, hopefully paying for tickets in advance; this will help get the money in faster. People can buy this historic club's merchandise either online or when at the club.

There is a sponsorship form available to download for those who want to raise money through events. One little girl 'Hannah' who is a fan has emptied her piggybank and given the money to the club, so they are saying it all helps. Businesses can donate money and get involved in fundraising activities, as well as coming to the games with customers or advertising their business at the club.

EXAMINER'S COMMENT

A good start to the set of answers, and a good start to this particular answer – the club has no money, so it needs some! It's a fairly efficient response all the way through, and I counted 11 points which are well organized.

Student response Question 2

The campaign clearly outlines how everyone can be involved in helping Accrington Stanley Football Club raise the money it needs. It appeals not just to the football fans and followers of the club, but businesses and individuals, both adults and children. The website makes it easy to donate money by showing that it accepts all payments on card, cash, PayPal and even shows that emptied piggybanks are acceptable and gratefully received.

The campaign is honest and shows why they need the money to pay a tax bill, not anything else. It asks businesses to get involved with 'hospitality visits, match day tickets, sponsorships and advertising'. It lists very clearly 4 'SOS' ways to help. Fans can bring friends to game and buy tickets in advance, buy merchandise which is open to everyone. Accrington Stanley is described as a 'historic football club', which is well-worded.

EXAMINER'S COMMENT

This is another good answer, but it's a rather harder question, so there is scope for improvement. The answer needs to be a little more focused on persuasive techniques and maybe more focused on the different types of people that might cough up some money! The answer discusses soundly the strengths of the campaign, but misses opportunities to focus on persuasion, especially in relation to the design of the pages, such as the pictures and lay-out.

Student response Question 3

The title of the article immediately shows how the writer feels when it says 'Manchester City is making a mockery of the game'. The writer is clearly unimpressed and goes on to say very strongly that 'their wild excess in the transfer market won't buy them any friends or win them any respect'. The writer is critical about some clubs' ability to buy any footballer without much thought to what is happening in the economy of the rest of the country. Whilst 'employers are all having to scale right back' this club continues to spend ridiculous money 'rocketing through the £200 million barrier since Hughes took over'. The writer thinks 'mega-rich' City is leading football to sign players for whatever it takes money wise and it is not realistic. It is also not acceptable to think this way when the rest of the country suffers.

EXAMINER'S COMMENT

Another good answer, which clearly picks up to some extent on the writer's strength of feeling. Sometimes writers are very subtle in their attitudes to the subject they are writing about, but here the journalist is a upset by the amount of money that goes to waste and the answer needs to reflect that. Some of the quotations here are a little too long; a short phrase like 'wild excess' could be used to illustrate irresponsibility. Alternatively, some comment should have been made on the longer quotation, as it stands. A little more confidence in focusing the argument would take this answer into the highest grade band.

Manchester City and Accrington Stanley Football clubs could not be more different. Clearly one has far too much money and the other needs money to stay alive. Whilst Manchester City spends '£200 million', Accrington Stanley is trying everything possible to raise £308,000 to pay a tax bill.

Accrington Stanley is calling on the help of loyal fans to the club and football fans everywhere to help them, by being honest and straightforward in its appeal on the website. Accrington Stanley's appeal also highlights how much fans think of the club when 'Hannah Holland has emptied her piggybank to help save' the club and how grateful the club are to her by giving her a seat in the directors' box as a thank you.

Manchester City are not thinking of normal people or fans at all, when they continue to spend, spend, spend 'while many fans struggle to rake together enough cash to be able to afford tickets'. The club are proving how 'they are completely out of step with the rest of us' when they pay £25 million for one player and then immediately pay it out again for another.

EXAMINER'S COMMENT

This answer completes a very good set of responses from our candidate. It's a clear, coherent response, giving the reader every chance to tick points made. But does it truly focus on 'different' and 'images'? Although it is a good commentary, sharper analysis is needed for top marks.

Exam Practice 2

Source text A

'Glad to have been a Girl Guide'
The Girl Guides reached its 100th birthday in 2009. This article from *The Independent* celebrates its place in British life.

Glad to have been a Girl Guide

It is 100 years since girls stormed a Boy Scout jamboree, demanding to join in. The Guides have come a long way since then, reports Rachel Shields

Sunday, 23 August 2009

As breeding grounds for talent go, it could give the country's top girls' schools a run for their money, counting JK Rowling, Dame Kelly Holmes and Emma Thompson among its former members.

Unlike those venerable institutions, however, the organisation that has helped to mould the characters of some of the nation's most successful women is often dismissed as a harmless pastime for middle-class white girls. Now, as the Girlguiding movement approaches its centenary, the organisation is keen to ditch its twee image and embrace the modern world.

The organisation has spent the past two years trying to boost its 600,000-strong membership – and drag the organisation firmly into the 21st century – using an outreach programme called the "Switch" project to recruit young women who would never normally set foot in a Girl Guide meeting; everyone from teenage mothers to girls from conservative Muslim families.

"We have more than half a million members, but there will be 11 million children in the country next year, so obviously we could be serving more girls," said Denise King, chief executive of Girlguiding UK.

The traditional "character-building" activities for which the movement was famed, such as learning to tie knots, put up tents and administer first aid, have been expanded in order to appeal to girls with different interests.

A group of young mums in Nelson, Norfolk, learned to cook cheap meals on a budget, complete an NSPCC course on keeping children safe, and were taught how to plan affordable day trips for youngsters. Even the classic Girl Guide badges – which for years were proudly displayed on blue sashes, after being painstakingly sewn on by diligent mothers – have been expanded and updated to cover more political topics.

At some groups with a lot of Muslim members, girls work towards the new "Right To" badge, which teaches them about their right to be heard, to express their feelings and to worship.

"Usually we don't get the opportunity to join groups, so it is nice to be able to hang out with other girls without my parents worrying about boys being there" said 15-year-old Amani Khan, who attends a Middlesbrough Guide group. "They are generally quite protective, and it was nice to be able to make new friends and build my self-confidence."

Creating a female-only space in which girls can feel comfortable trying new things has always been one of the main objectives of the Guide movement.

Next month 7,000 Girl Guides will gather at Crystal Palace, south London, the spot where in 1909 girls in makeshift uniforms stormed a Boy Scout meeting and demanded that a group be created for them, to celebrate the organisation.

When Robert Baden-Powell, who went on to found the Girl Guides, wrote Scouting for Boys in 1908, he noted that: "Girls as well as boys may well learn scouting when young, and so be able to do useful work in the world when they are older". With a quick survey of former Guides turning up an Olympic gold medallist, a leading politician, an award-winning actress and a best-selling author, it looks as if he may well have been on to something.

Emma Thompson, *Actress*
The former Girl Guide and Oscar-winning actress believes that through the organisation "girls and young women can gain the confidence to be equal partners and to make informed, responsible choices about their lives". Thompson is now working with the Guides again, on a project which encourages them to become 'Climate Champions', reducing carbon emissions by advocating solar panels, switching off appliances and properly insulating homes. "Becoming a Climate Champion will enable girls and young women to take effective action on climate change – the biggest challenge the planet faces," she says.

Dame Kelly Holmes, *Athlete*
The Olympic champion says attending Girl Guide meetings in Kent taught her to "be the best you can be". It seems that the gold medal winner is now inspiring others to reach their full potential, with a recent survey of Girl Guides revealing that 86 per cent of them believe Dame Kelly to be the country's best female role model.

JK Rowling, *Author*
The Harry Potter author, who attended Brownies and Guides in Scotland, thinks Hermione Granger would make a good Guide: "I can easily imagine her in the Guides, given that she's resourceful, highly motivated and eager to learn. She might be a little over-competitive when it came to badges, though." She says her proudest guiding memory was bagging her First Aid badge: "I've never needed to make a sling since, but I'm on constant standby".

Source text B

'Should girls be allowed in the Boy Scouts?'
This blog by a young American argues for a mixed-gender scouting movement in the name of equality.

```
● ● ○                                      girlguides.blogspot
◄ ► + ⊕ http://girlguides.blogspot                              ↻  Q▾ Google
⊡ ▦                                                                      YouTube        »
      girlguides.blogspot                                                               +
```

Should girls be allowed in the Boy Scouts?

by Stace Fielding

Shouldn't it be called just "the scouts"? Aren't we supposed to be equal now?

Rock climbing and orienteering isn't just for boys; cookery and needlework isn't just for girls. The only splitting of the sexes should be in bathrooms and locker rooms. Otherwise, we're all in this world together and we can work, play and learn together. The whole principle of the scouts should be helping each other – not restricting a movement to 50% of the children who may want to be a part of it.

Calling an organisation "Boy Scouts" is immediately setting up beliefs and barriers in the minds of the young and vulnerable. Boys should be taught that their sisters are as adventurous as they are – no, they shouldn't need to be taught that, they should be able to SEE that all around them. Similarly, girls should never be excluded from anything because of their gender, and they should never be allowed to think that that is even a possibility.

In the newly unisex Scouts, I would initiate a programme of activities that boys and girls could work together on. Not just sports but skills and crafts that are needed in life – why shouldn't it be drummed into boys that they can cook, clean rooms and wash dishes just as girls can drive, build walls and (when older) shoot targets?

Yes, to call an organisation the "boy scouts" is sexist in itself; to actively encourage boys and not girls to join is horrible. It's denying half the kids of America the right to participate in organised activities.

People say "well there's the girl scouts or the girl guides" (I prefer the latter title because it suggests that girls are 'guiding' boys), but their program isn't full of the outdoor activities of the boys'.

No, I think that anyone who denies girls the chance to join the boy scout association is demonstrating an old-fashioned outlook. And in case anyone's worried about girls and boys working together – well, in my experience, security is paramount when it comes to games and camping. What I mean is that the girls would never be in a vulnerable position.

When my brother went camping with his scout troop it was a mixed sex affair. The girls (who made up a third of the group) had female supervisors and their own bathroom and shower facilities. I remember my little brother complaining that the girls had "doors on their stalls" (and I scolded him for even knowing that!), but it proved that the girls were being catered for.

So there really isn't an argument here, is there? Could anyone find a reason for girls NOT being admitted to the "boy scouts"? Yes, I'm sure a man could IF he tried! But no one in the modern world SHOULD be trying to.

This answer needs to be organized clearly point by point. There does not have to be explicit comparison on every point, but there needs to be clear signalling regarding the changes.

*Answer **all** the following questions.*

Look at 'Glad to have been a Girl Guide'.

1. In what ways has the Girl Guides changed in the 100 years since it was first formed?   [10]

2. What is the attitude of the writer to the Girl Guides?   [10]

Now look at 'Should girls be allowed in the Boy Scouts?'

3. How does Stace Fielding try to persuade the reader that girls should be allowed to join the Boy Scouts?   [10]

    Think about: what she says and how she says it.

To answer the next question, you need to look at both texts.

4. Using information from both texts, explain how successful you think the Girl Guides have been in keeping up with modern life.
                                                                  [10]

The critical thing here is to start with a worked-out position, which should not be too difficult. The attitude does not exactly shift, but there are some reflections beyond general support.

Stace is quite clever because she is using fundamental equality arguments in a fairly uncompromising way. She is not hot-headed, but she is assertive.

This is quite a difficult question, because you have to weigh up the views of two opposing writers, without necessarily agreeing strongly with either.

Sample answers

Here is a set of answers written by one student followed by comments from the examiner.

Student response Question 1

The Girl Guides formed 100 years ago with girls in makeshift uniforms wanting to be part of something. Now, with proper uniforms and members worldwide it is a modern day organization which has changed to move into the 21st century. Previously thought of as 'a harmless pastime for middle-class white girls', the Girl Guides introduced an outreach programme called 'switch project' to attract young women who would never step into a guide meeting to join, attracting teenage mothers and young Muslim girls. They recognized the need to change with their Chief Executive being aware that 'obviously we could be serving more girls'. They have changed the exercises they do to include budgeting, cooking on a budget, NSPCC childcare as well as the more traditional first aid. There are also new badges available on updated topics and recognition of multicultural society in a 'Right to' badge to enable Muslim women to learn their rights and increase confidence. It is still a girl-only group which allows freedom of speech and a level of security, which will not change.

EXAMINER'S COMMENT

The above answer eventually gets moving by making points about the modern organization, but it starts slowly by recalling the past and the changes. That's a different question, not the one that is asked here! The first point that the student makes refers to the introduction of the outreach programme and there is no reference at all in the answer to the celebrities who are happy to speak up for the Girl Guides. There is a good opportunity here to select and organize a more complete, balanced response.

Student response Question 2

Rachel Shields, the writer, shows her enthusiasm and respect for the Girl Guide movement. she recognizes that since the original girls stormed the Boy Scout jamboree 100 years ago the movement has been progressively addressing the needs of guides and young women and changing in many ways to constantly move with the times. The writer also recognizes the introduction of new activities and badges that allow more modern skills to be learnt, and political and social needs of the twenty-first century to be addressed. Muslim girls from 'conservative' families are being taught a 'Right to' badge, which teaches them about freedom of speech and their own rights, which is all very positive. The writer obviously realizes that the guides movement needed to change and 'ditch its twee image' and that when it was initially established the whole idea was to allow girls to do 'useful work in the world when they are older' which was an old-fashioned viewpoint.

EXAMINER'S COMMENT

This answer is a good one; the student definitely starts confidently by identifying the writer's 'enthusiasm and respect' and supports this with phrases like 'progressively addressing', 'allow more modern skills' and 'which is all very positive'. The answer could be a little more explicit on the gentle criticisms expressed by the writer, but the answer remains focused on the question throughout.

Student response Question 3

The opening lines of Stace Fielding's article outline exactly what the article will be about and how it will be written 'Aren't we supposed to be equal now?' the writer constantly emphasizes this throughout. Why should sports activities and cooking be separate through the sexes? The point of scouting is 'helping each other' not disallowing girls to be part of it. The writer believes that the 'Boy Scouts' name sets up barriers that should not exist in the modern world and is sexist in itself. Everyone should be included, taught the same things, taught skills and crafts that are useful in the world, not just for boys or girls but for everyone.

The writer is very conscious that it is old-fashioned to restrict girls joining, camps can be controlled without any concerns about security. Very adamantly at the end the writer says there is no argument to girls being allowed to join scouts and 'no one in the modern world' should be saying there is.

EXAMINER'S COMMENT

In this case, the answer is a bit hasty at the start. Stace Fielding starts with two questions (three if you include the headline), so how can we 'see exactly what the article is about'? As the answer progresses, there are some useful comments on the content of the article, but little attention is paid to the 'how?' in the question, that is the ways the writer goes about trying to persuade the reader. Although comments such as 'constantly emphasizes', 'very conscious', and 'very adamantly' do show an awareness of the writer, there are some obvious points to tackle, including those questions at the start and the tone that they set.

Student response Question 4

Both articles agree with the usefulness of the Girl Guides and the skills it teaches. The second article just wants a mixed-sex group to allow all skills to be taught without discrimination against gender. Both articles highlight the need to move forward and be in the modern world. The Girl Guides have introduced an 'outreach programme' to recruit everyone from teenage mothers to Muslim women thus increasing the diversity of the movement. The second article takes this another step by asking for just one movement to include both boys and girls, allowing all skills and crafts to be taught to everyone. This also teaches equality.

The Girl Guides have changed activities and badges to fit into society now. They have kept the traditional values but also moved onto to teach budgeting childcare, cooking and have looked at racial equality in a 'Right to' badge for young Muslim girls to understand their rights in society. They have famous people involved to highlight causes like 'climate champion' Emma Thompson, encouraging responsibility. Both articles believe that teaching these skills and the idea of belonging to a group is fundamental to its success and both agree that the need to constantly change and update is essential.

EXAMINER'S COMMENT

The answer is clear in the points it makes sentence by sentence, and it deals evenly with both texts. It appears to be taking the view that both writers are equally effective in their arguments, which is valid, but rather cautious. More importantly, it is harder to do! Examiners strongly advise that with an evaluation question like this one that you do state a preference by the end of your answer at the very least. Another strong piece of advice is: use the bullet points in the question to organize your answer. Comparison questions need focused, balanced answers.

How is non-fiction reading assessed at GCSE?

Use the questions below to check the level of your own performance. See if you can measure your progress through the chapter.

Questions on locating and selecting detail (Question 1)

This kind of question tests the skills of reading and understanding texts, and **selecting material** appropriate to purpose.

Are there…
- ☐ simple comments with occasional reference to the text, or non-selective copying?
- ☐ simple comments based on surface features of the text and/or some awareness of more obvious implicit meanings?
- ☐ valid comments/inferences based on appropriate detail from the text?
- ☐ valid comments/inferences and exploration of the text in detail and specific detail combined with overview?

Questions on writers' ideas and perspectives (Question 2)

This kind of question tests the ability to read and understand texts, and select material appropriate to purpose, and **develop and sustain an interpretation of writers' ideas and perspectives**.

Are there…
- ☐ unsupported assertions and simple comments with occasional references to the text?
- ☐ appropriate references to the text with some comment?
- ☐ appropriate details from the text, which begin to address the issue of 'how', but with some 'spotting and listing' of key words or quotations?
- ☐ valid points selected and explained, with some depth of understanding and overview?

Questions on persuasion (Question 3)

This kind of question tests the skills of reading and understanding texts, and selecting material appropriate to purpose. It also tests **how writers use linguistic, grammatical, structural and presentational features**.

Are there…
- ☐ unsupported assertions and simple comments with occasional references to the text?
- ☐ appropriate references to the text with simple comments/inferences?
- ☐ valid comments based on appropriate detail from the text, which begin to address the issue of 'how', but with some 'spotting and listing' of key words or quotations?
- ☐ valid comments/inferences, which combine specific detail with overview and are fully engaged with analysis of techniques?

Questions on comparison (Question 4)

This kind of question tests the ability to select material appropriate to purpose, to collate material from different sources and **make comparisons and cross-references as appropriate**.

Are there...
- ❑ unsupported assertions and simple comments with occasional references to the text?
- ❑ some clear, if obvious, comparisons and contrasts?
- ❑ some valid cross-references expressed and organized satisfactorily?
- ❑ coherent and perceptive comments, ranging confidently across both texts?

Preparing for the exam

Here are the relevant details from the GCSE specifications from this part of the assessment, including the Assessment Objectives for each specification (these are the skills you are trying to show to gain marks and grades).

GCSE ENGLISH LANGUAGE UNIT 1: Studying written language

Reading: non-fiction texts (20%)

Examination

You will complete structured questions on **two** non-fiction texts. The exam lasts for 1 hour.

AO3 Studying written language

- Read and understand texts, selecting material appropriate to purpose, collating from different sources and making comparisons and cross-references as appropriate.
- Develop and sustain interpretations of writers' ideas and perspectives.
- Explain and evaluate how writers use linguistic, grammatical, structural and presentational features to achieve effects and engage and influence the reader.
- Understand texts in their social, cultural and historical contexts.

GCSE ENGLISH UNIT 1: English in the daily world (reading)

Reading: non-fiction texts (20%)

Examination

You will complete structured questions on **two** non-fiction texts. The exam lasts for 1 hour.

AO2 Reading

- Read and understand texts, selecting material appropriate to purpose, collating from different sources and making comparisons and cross-references as appropriate.
- Develop and sustain interpretations of writers' ideas and perspectives.
- Explain and evaluate how writers use linguistic, grammatical, structural and presentational features to achieve effects and engage and influence the reader.
- Understand texts in their social, cultural and historical contexts.

Before the day

- Revise different text types to cover those which might appear in the exam.
- Read as many relevant 'past papers' and 'specimen papers' as you can.
- Practice individual questions 'against the clock' (12–13 minutes) as well as whole papers.
- Identify the key words in questions, such as those which ask you to consider writers' attitudes and perspectives, and persuasive techniques.

On the day

- Weigh up both texts and the questions – read quickly but purposefully.
- Get a sense of the audience and purpose of each text.
- Work out the writer's attitudes in each of the texts.
- Annotate as you read and underline key words.
- Focus closely on what each question is asking – is it a '**how**' or a '**what**' question?
- Spend more or less equal time on each question (12–13 minutes each).
- Write answers of more or less equal length.
- Do not miss out any questions!

GCSE English Literature Unit 1 Section B

In Section B of the Unit 1 exam, you will have to complete a question comparing two contemporary **unseen** poems.

Unseen... Poetry... Comparison... Each word can provoke some uncertainty in the minds of literature students, but without any real cause.

Unseen means that you need to apply your reading skills as you would normally do when you are reading something for the first time. The poem will not be impossible to understand! **Poetry** requires you to be thoughtful and sensitive in response. It is shaped differently on the page, but you should still read it for meaning, sentence-by-sentence. **Comparison** simply means that you will be looking at two poems rather than one and making connections between the two where they occur to you.

This chapter is divided into three stages for you to cover:
1. a poetry comparison with plenty of structure and support
2. a second pair of poems with some guidance provided
3. a third task for you to tackle independently.

You should adopt a questioning approach to your reading of poetry. Do not fall into the trap of thinking there is a perfect explanation, and do not make yourself dependent on your teacher for the 'expert' answer; remember that how you respond to the 'unseen' is part of what you are being assessed on in the exam and you will need to build your confidence.

1. Poetry comparison: full support

In the exam the Comparative Study will be presented as follows:

SECTION B

Spend about 1 hour on this section. Think carefully about the poems before you write your answer.

6.   Both of the following poems are about nature and climate. *Hurricane* has a tropical setting, while *Autumn* is a British poem.
   Write about both poems and their effect on you. Show how they are similar and how they are different.
   You may write about each poem separately and then compare them, or make comparisons where appropriate in your answer as a whole.

You may wish to include some or all of these points:

- *the content of the poems – what they are about;*
- *the ideas the poets may have wanted us to think about;*
- *the mood or atmosphere of the poems;*
- *how they are written – words and phrases you find interesting, the way they are organized, and so on;*
- *your responses to the poems.*   [20]

Hurricane

Under low black clouds
the wind was all
speedy feet, all horns and breath,
all bangs, howls, rattles,
5   in every hen house,
church hall and school.

Roaring, screaming, returning,
it made forced entry, shoved walls,
made rifts, brought roofs down,
10   hitting rooms to sticks apart.

It wrung soft banana trees,
broke tough trunks of palms.
It pounded vines of yams,
left fields battered up.

15   Invisible with such ecstasy
with no intervention of sun or man –
everywhere kept changing branches.

Zinc sheets are kites.
Leaves are panic swarms.
20   Fowls are fixed with feathers turned.
Goats, dogs, pigs,
all are people together.

Then growling it slunk away
from muddy, mossy trail and boats
25   in hedges and cows, ratbats, trees,
fish, all dead in the road.

James Berry

Autumn

Autumn arrives
Like an experienced robber
Grabbing the green stuff
Then cunningly covering his tracks
5 With a deep multitude
Of colourful distractions.
And the wind,
The wind is his accomplice
Putting an air of chaos
10 Into the careful diversions
So branches shake
And dead leaves are suddenly blown
In the faces of inquisitive strangers.
The theft chills the world
15 Changes the temper of the earth
Till the normally placid sky grows red with a quiet rage.

Alan Bold

When completing the exam, read the poems with your pen in your hand and annotate
the poem on your exam paper as you go. Annotation means adding short notes and
explanations to a text, in this case a poem. You can use this technique to sort out your
thoughts on the poems. For example,

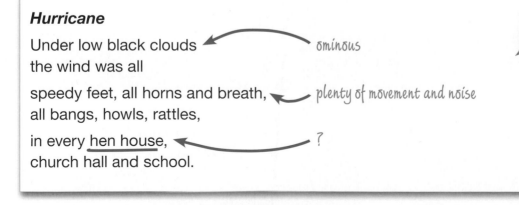

Hurricane

Under low black clouds ⟵ *ominous*
the wind was all

speedy feet, all horns and breath, ⟵ *plenty of movement and noise*
all bangs, howls, rattles,

in every hen house, ⟵ *?*
church hall and school.

Read both poems, taking the structure and punctuation into account.

Then try to identify the **voice** and the **situation** of each poem. Voice and situation are key starting points for understanding a poem. Who is speaking in the poem? Is it a first-person speaker or a third-person narrator (he/she)? What is the tone of voice? Excited? Controlled? Angry? Sad? Are you able to state the situation at the start of the poem in straightforward terms?

1   **In 'Hurricane' the voice is that of someone observing the hurricane or reporting its damage. There is a sweeping survey of a village, but no apparent emotional attachment and no people. Is there anything else you notice?**
2   **Read 'Autumn' for voice and situation.**
    ■   **Is the voice similar to, or is it very different from the voice in 'Hurricane'?**
    ■   **There is a definite situation and setting in 'Hurricane', but not in 'Autumn'. What can you add generally about the scene in 'Autumn' at this stage of your reading?**
3   **Now look again at the opening (lines 1-6) of 'Hurricane'. What is happening in these six lines?**

Read on and answer the questions about 'Hurricane' considering each sentence in sequence.

Lines 7-10:

■   **How does the poet make the hurricane seem threatening?**
■   **Comment on the use of the underlined words below.**

It <u>wrung</u> soft banana trees,
<u>broke</u> tough trunks of palms.
It <u>pounded</u> vines of yams,
left fields <u>battered</u> up.

Lines 15-17:
- Explain what is happening in these three lines. What does 'Invisible with such ecstasy' mean?

Lines 18-20:
- Comment on the imagery in these lines.

Lines 21-22:
- What is the effect of these two lines?

Lines 23-26:
- Comment on the effect of the underlined items in the lines below.

  Then <u>growling</u> it <u>slunk</u> away
  from muddy, mossy trail and <u>boats</u>
  <u>in hedges</u>: and <u>cows, ratbats, trees,</u>
  <u>fish, all dead in the road</u>.

Imagery

An image in poetry (or writing generally) is a picture created in the mind of the reader by the words used.

On a simple **descriptive** level, **literal** images can be effective, for example, 'under low black clouds'. The reader sees these things in an uncomplicated way.

Similes and **metaphors** are non-literal or **figurative** images. They are often used to put more challenging images into your mind. They are images built upon **comparisons** and these are often unusual and thought-provoking. A **simile** is an **indirect comparison** using 'like' or 'as' to link one thing to the other. A **metaphor** is a **direct comparison**, often using 'is' to make the clearest possible association.

'Zinc sheets are kites' = metaphor
'Autumn arrives like an experienced robber' = simile

It really does not matter if you cannot distinguish between the different types of images or if you cannot remember any of the technical terms. What matters is that you can respond to the words of the poem in a thoughtful, sensitive way.

Now look again at 'Autumn'. It is a shorter poem than 'Hurricane', so ensure you develop your comments fully. Make comparisons with 'Hurricane' as you go along.

Lines 1-6:
- Explain fully the situation as it is described in the opening sentence of the poem. How different is the tone of voice in this poem from the voice of the narrator in 'Hurricane'?

> **Lines 7-13:**
>
> ■ **Explore the poet's choice of words and phrases in these lines. How does he convey the climate? How does it compare with conditions in the previous poem?**
>
> **Lines 14-16:**
>
> ■ **Explore the language used by the poet at the end of the poem. How effective is the ending of this short poem in your opinion? How does it compare with the ending of 'Hurricane'?**

In your responses to the questions above, you should have produced enough material for a sound answer to a GCSE exam question. Now look at one person's response to the task. You could use some of this and some of your own ideas to write a response to the two poems.

The poem 'Hurricane' is a report, a commentary, a description of a hurricane. The poet is an observer and spectator; he is present as a witness, but it appears that he is detached and personally not in distress or in danger.

It is a tropical, scene, with hen houses and tropical fruits, no humans but lots of creatures at the mercy of the hurricane. There is panic, suggested by 'all speedy feet' and noisy chaos with 'bangs, howls, rattles'.

The hurricane is violent, angry and noisy. 'Roaring, screaming, returning, it made forced entry'. It does its damage in a bad-tempered way 'left fields battered up' before eventually 'growling it slunk away'. The violence is actually quite shocking with the verbs 'wrung', 'broke', 'pounded'.

However, 'invisible with such ecstasy' suggests something different, a poltergeist out of control, wreaking havoc and enjoying it, teasing and scaring those in its path. 'Everywhere kept changing branches' is confusing for the reader, but again it suggests violent movement and things dislocated.

The language is actually quite simple. It is quite easy to imagine the roofs flying ('Zinc sheets are kites') and the bits and pieces swirling ('Leaves are panic swarms').

It appears that humans did not die in this hurricane but animals did. The hurricane departs, almost as quickly as it came, as if we are wondering what the fuss was about. For us in Britain, it is probably out of our experience, but the tropical hurricane is a death machine. My favourite image is 'boats in hedges', which is just put simply, exactly as it says, not a metaphor or simile. The hurricane comes and goes, and leaves a trail of destruction.

You could say 'Autumn' by comparison is tame, but that is the strength of the wind talking, not the poem. 'Autumn' is light and witty, describing nothing more threatening than the leaves being blown from the trees of Britain. It is a regular event, an annual thing, represented as 'an experienced robber'. It is a clever metaphor to refer to the 'green stuff' (leaves/money) and giving the impression that autumn is not a natural process of change, but an elaborate theft by a team of conmen and thieves. To the end of the poem the metaphor of the thief is kept up, with all of the features of autumn, the leaves off the trees, the lowering temperatures and the angry red skies all represented in terms of criminals and victims.

The second poem is playful, but while the first one has some stark images that stop you in your tracks and almost make you laugh (for example, 'boats in hedges'), ultimately it has the extra impact of the tropical life-threatening hurricane. Both poems match the degree of seriousness of the scene, so they are both perfect in their way, but 'Hurricane' describes the out-of-the-ordinary, while 'Autumn' describes the familiar.

EXAMINER'S COMMENT

There are a lot of riches in the answer above. This answer has been written by someone who has done the reading coolly before composing the response and has positioned himself/herself properly in response to each poem. By starting in the right place, as it were, the student has properly unlocked the meaning of both poems and the comparisons come naturally and fluidly.

2. Poetry comparison: guided reading

SECTION B

Spend about 1 hour on this section. Think carefully about the poems before you write your answer.

6. Both of the following poems, *Morning* and *In Praise of the Great Bull Walrus*, are about animals and how we use them to explain life to ourselves.

   Write about both poems and their effect on you. Show how they are similar and how they are different.

   You may write about each poem separately and then compare them, or make comparisons where appropriate in your answer as a whole.

   You may wish to include some or all of these points:

   - *the content of the poems – what they are about;*
   - *the ideas the poets may have wanted us to think about;*
   - *the mood or atmosphere of the poems;*
   - *how they are written – words and phrases you find interesting, the way they are organized, and so on;*
   - *your responses to the poems.*   [20]

Morning

Salt shining behind its glass cylinder.
Milk in a blue bowl. The yellow linoleum.
The cat stretching her black body from the pillow.
The way she makes her curvaceous response to the small, kind gesture.
5 Then laps the bowl clean.
Then wants to go out into the world
where she leaps lightly and for no apparent reason across the lawn,
then sits, perfectly still, in the grass.
I watch her a little while, thinking:
10 what more could I do with wild words?
I stand in the cold kitchen, bowing down to her.
I stand in the cold kitchen, everything wonderful around me.

Mary Oliver

In Praise of the Great Bull Walrus

I wouldn't like to be one
of the walrus people
for the rest of my life
but I wish I could spend
5 one sunny afternoon
lying on the rocks with them.
I suspect it would be similar
to drinking beer in a tavern
that caters to longshoremen
10 and won't admit women.
We'd admit no
cosmic secrets. I'd merely say,
'How yuh doin' you big old walrus?'
and the nearest of
15 the walrus people
would answer,
'Me? I'm doin' great.
How yuh doin' yourself,
you big old human being, you?'
20 How good it is to share
the earth with such creatures
and how unthinkable it would have been
to have missed all this
by not being born:
25 a happy thought, that,
for not being born is
the only tragedy
that we can imagine
but never fear.

Alden Nowlan

'Morning'

First, look at the first poem in detail. 'Morning' is a brief, compact poem. Look at the first two lines, the next six lines, and the remaining two lines.

Content

- Consider the voice and situation, as established by the opening.
- Make sure you follow the development of the poem logically.
- Coverage - make sure you reach the end and cover the parts of the poem evenly.

Ideas

- What significance does the poet give to the simple domestic moment shared by the speaker and her cat?

Mood and atmosphere

- How does the poet create a positive mood and atmosphere?

How the poem is written

- Look closely at the poet's choice of words and phrases. Your selections and comments should be woven into your response, rather than treated as a separate section.
- The language of the poem is quite simple and clear, but some words, phrases and even sentences stand out. Make sure you have not missed good opportunities to comment.

Personal response

- You should be able to engage personally and positively to an everyday situation such as that described in the poem: morning, a kitchen, a cat.

'In Praise of the Great Bull Walrus'

Now look at the second poem, referring back when appropriate to the first poem and pointing out meaningful connections. Make sure you have given roughly equal treatment to each poem, even though they are poems of different length. Identify points of comparison between the two poems wherever these occur to you.

Content

- How is the voice different from the other poem right from the very start?
- Explain in your own words what the speaker/narrator/poet is imagining. Refer to the opening of the poem, the development, and the ending.

Ideas

■ **Expand if you can on the way the poet is using the image of the walruses basking on the rocks to reflect on life. Make links if you wish with the ideas in the other poem.**

Mood or atmosphere

■ **You may have already established the mood of this poem. Make links with the mood and atmosphere of 'Morning'.**

How the poem is written

■ **You may have identified interesting words and phrases to comment upon. In this poem it is not easy to pick out single words usefully.**

Personal response

■ **End with your personal response to 'In Praise of the Great Bull Walrus'. You should also make final comparisons with 'Morning'.**

EXAMINER'S TIP

■ When quoting, vary the length of your quotations, but keep them as short as possible, so they can be integrated into the flow of your writing. However, note that 'In Praise of the Great Bull Walrus' is not easy to quote from. You may need to lengthen your quotes in order for them to make good sense - for example, 'How good it is to share/the earth with such creatures' or 'a tavern that... won't admit women'. Be skilful with longer quotations.

Finally, conclude with any further comments about the differences and similarities between the two poems.

You now have an essay structure that could give you ten developed paragraphs. This is not essential, for you may have integrated features like mood or language elsewhere into your essay. However, you should try to ensure that your essay is organized and purposeful, and demonstrates your skills in responding to unseen poems.

Now read the following sample answer.

'Morning' by Mary Oliver and 'In Praise of the Great Bull Walrus' by Alden Nowlan

'Morning' is an interesting poem written clearly through the eyes of a cat lover. The title gives nothing away to tell you what the poem is about and only when you reach the third line is the cat shown to be the main character: 'The cat stretching her black body from the pillow'. The cat is shown to be a spoilt creature whose characteristics are shown clearly throughout the lines, for example 'leaps lightly' and 'laps the bowl clean'.

The writer enjoys watching the animal and has respect for the creature, this is shown when she says 'bowing down to her'.

The language is descriptive and you can imagine very clearly what the surroundings are in the house, 'the yellow linoleum' and 'cold kitchen'. The writer describes the cat and how simple the life is when you are fed and grateful and then can go and play in the garden. The writer also spends time thinking about the animal and the life it has. The writer also then thinks about how nice her own life is when she writes the line 'everything wonderful around me'.

When you look at 'In Praise of the Great Bull Walrus', another animal is being described in a different way, through a human eye and conversation rather than describing the animal and its features.

The writer has watched the Bull Walrus lying on the rocks in the sun and although he 'wouldn't like to be one' he does recognize their happy existence on the rocks. The writer then makes the poem into a conversation that men would have in a 'tavern' whilst having a beer. He makes the walruses seem human in a different way to the first poem with the cat and its human qualities. The men are talking to each other and referring to each other as 'you big old walrus'

The writer in this poem considers 'how good it is to share the earth with such creatures' and his gladness to be here on earth to see it. This shows similarities with the first poem in that both writers are enjoying being alive and seeing what these animals offer.

The poems are similar in lots of ways particularly in that they are both about animals and the ways that the animal's simple enjoyment of things can reflect on humans and the way they think about life.

The differences are mainly in how they are written, with the first one being descriptive about the cat and watching it go about everyday things, whilst the second has more on human reference. Both are linked to each writer's love of animals.

EXAMINER'S COMMENT

This is a fluent, methodical response of quite good length. However, there is a little bit of wishful thinking in some of the comments. After all, the cat is not really spoiled, though it might have an easy life. Equally, the walruses do not necessarily represent the writer's love of animals. Some of the points are rather superficial and general, as if the cat and walruses are having a really good time in a way that humans don't. However, the point is well made that humans have something to learn from animals.

3. Poetry Comparison: Exam Practice

With the final pair of poems, complete the task using only the bullet-point support offered in the exam. Remember to structure your response in the ways that you have practised. Remember also to think positively about your reading skills.

SECTION B

Spend about 1 hour on this section. Think carefully about the poems before you write your answer.

6. Both of the following poems are about old age. *Handbag* looks back, while *Warning* looks forward.

    Write about both poems and their effect on you. Show how they are similar and how they are different.

    You may write about each poem separately and then compare them, or make comparisons where appropriate in your answer as a whole.

    You may wish to include some or all of these points:

    -   *the content of the poems – what they are about;*
    -   *the ideas the poets may have wanted us to think about;*
    -   *the mood or atmosphere of the poems;*
    -   *how they are written – words and phrases you find interesting, the way they are organized, and so on;*
    -   *your responses to the poems.*   [20]

    ### Handbag

    My mother's old leather handbag,
    crowded with letters she carried
    all through the war. The smell
    of my mother's handbag: mints
    and lipstick and Coty powder.
    The look of those letters, softened
    and worn at the edges, opened,
    read, and refolded so often.
    Letters from my father. Odour
    of leather and powder, which ever
    since then has meant womanliness,
    and love, and anguish, and war.

    Ruth Fainlight

Warning

When I am an old woman I shall wear purple
With a red hat which doesn't go, and doesn't suit me.
And I shall spend my pension on brandy and summer gloves
And satin sandals, and say we've no money for butter.
I shall sit down on the pavement when I'm tired
And gobble up samples in shops and press alarm bells
And run my stick along the public railings
And make up for the sobriety of my youth.
I shall go out in my slippers in the rain
And pick the flowers in other people's gardens
And learn to spit.

You can wear terrible shirts and grow more fat
And eat three pounds of sausages at a go
Or only bread and pickle for a week
And hoard pens and pencils and beermats and things in boxes.

But now we must have clothes that keep us dry
And pay our rent and not swear in the street
And set a good example for the children.
We must have friends to dinner and read the papers.

But maybe I ought to practise a little now?
So people who know me are not too shocked and surprised
When suddenly I am old, and start to wear purple.

Jenny Joseph

How is the unseen poetry comparison assessed at GCSE?

Coverage of poems
- ❏ Are there simple, general comments on the poems?
- ❏ Is there some discussion and awareness of the mood, atmosphere, and themes of the poems?
- ❏ Is there focused and thoughtful discussion of the detail of both poems?
- ❏ Is there assured appreciation and analysis of both poems?

Comparisons
- ❏ Are there simple and basic points of comparison?
- ❏ Is there some discussion and awareness of similarities and differences?
- ❏ Are there clear points of comparison made?
- ❏ Are there confident and appropriate links and comparisons?

Read the sample answer below.

Sample answer
Read the sample student answer below followed by comments from the examiner.

Student response

'Handbag' and 'Warning'

'Handbag' is a poem that describes an 'old leather handbag' which the writer's mother has carried with her since the war. The descriptions of the contents of the handbag are poignant as they relate to the lady's life and what she has been through. The writer describes the contents with fondness and love which gives the poem warmth even though it is sad at the same time. 'The smell of my mother's handbag: mints and lipstick and Coty powder' conjure up images of how the handbag looks and you can smell the items as you are reading the lines. When reading you get a sense of the women whose handbag it is, even though she is not described at all and no age is given. The memory of the war and the hardship of being alone also comes through the lines describing the letters she carries with her 'softened and worn at the edges', these words seem to not only describe the letters but also seem to describe the women as she gets older and the love she had in her life which is tinged with sorrow.

The second poem 'Warning' is also about old age but is written expressing how the writer will be when she gets old and the things she will do. The poem is amusing as you can see the humour in the terrible things the writer wants to do, which is to rebel against what society expects of old people. And also she realises that at this point on her life she must stick to society's rules: 'But now we must have clothes that keep us dry/And pay our rent and not swear in the street'.

It is as if the writer is looking forward to being able to rebel and do the things we cannot do now, but that old age will release her from that, as she will be seen as old and eccentric so may just get away with it: 'You can wear terrible shirts and grow more fat'.

The image of the character wearing purple and 'with a red hat which doesn't go' is an image of a funny, slightly mad character which is a stark comparison to the lady in the first poem where old age is a sad, lonely existence. The lady in 'Warning' will not be sad but will be enjoying her old age.

Although both poems are about getting old and the ways we change, they are very different. I prefer the second poem 'Warning' as the humour and fun make me enjoy reading it, rather than feeling sadness and a wish not to get old from 'handbag'. If we could all view aging in the way of the second writer, it would seem more fun.

EXAMINER'S COMMENT

There is a good level of natural, personal response here, enough to take the student into the higher bands of the assessment criteria. In the first poem, the student could have got closer to the drama of the situation, in which presumably the daughter of the woman looks back across time, back to the war years and imagines her mother then. In other words, the poem is not just about the feeling of melancholy. Again, in the second poem, the voice is critical and could have been analysed a little more.

Preparing for the exam

Here are the relevant details from the GCSE specification for this part of the assessment, including the relevant Assessment Objectives for the specifications.

GCSE ENGLISH LITERATURE UNIT 1 Section B: poetry (contemporary)
Comparative study (14%)

Examination

For this section of the exam, you will answer **one** question comparing two contemporary unseen poems. Both poems will be printed on the question paper and the question will also include a number of bullet-point prompts to help you structure your answer. In order to prepare for this part of the exam, you will study at least fifteen poems in addition to those studied for Unit 3 of English Literature.

AO1

- Respond to texts critically and imaginatively; select and evaluate relevant textual detail to illustrate and support interpretations.

AO2

- Explain how language, structure and form contribute to writers' presentation of ideas, themes and settings.

AO3

- Make comparisons and explain links between texts, evaluating writers' different ways of expressing meaning and achieving effects.

Before the day

- Read as many poems as you can, especially from past papers and specimen papers. Work out how you would tackle each one in an exam.
- Train yourself to weigh up how to cover poems of different lengths.
- Practise how to begin a response, positioning yourself to make sensible comments about the start of the poem.
- Get used to using the language like 'perhaps', 'possibly' and 'maybe' to show that you appreciate that poetry can be interpreted in different ways.
- Practise a cautious approach to technical language, avoiding empty, meaningless comments.
- Get a sound approach to comparison, above all avoiding ping-pong between the two poems!
- Build your confidence when making personal comments in response to poems.

On the day

- Make sure you leave yourself a full hour for this part of the exam.
- Read with your pen in your hand, annotating as you go along.
- Make sure that you read, think about, and prepare both poems before you start to write your answer.
- Use the bullet-point support at the top of the exam paper, either as a checklist or as a structure for your response.
- Write about the first poem coherently at some length, then write about the second poem with references back where you feel fit.
- Make cautious 'overview' comments on both poems, based on the ideas that you think the poets are leaving you with.

Making effective annotations

1. Before you begin reading and thinking about the poems in your exam, you might find it useful to circle or highlight the key words of the question. This will help you to focus your attention on what you should look for as you read the poems.

2. As you read the poems, be prepared to highlight or circle any phrases that stand out. These phrases might convey images or feelings that have a particular impact on you – helping you to form your 'personal response'. Alternatively, you might notice something that relates directly to the wording in the question, something that you will definitely want to refer to when you come to write your answer.

3. As well as circling or highlighting features, jot down your thoughts quickly in the margin. Write something that will prompt you when you come back to write about the poem in your answer. Usually a quick question or a couple of key words is all you need. Keep your notes brief and aim to expand on them in your answer.

4. When you read the second poem, try to identify links as you go along and annotate these too.

5. Once you have read both poems, you can number your notes in the order that you would like to write about them, prioritizing your best ideas and connecting points that are related. This will help you to structure your response effectively.

GCSE English Literature Unit 3

For Unit 3 you will be required to produce a written assignment linking a play by Shakespeare with a group of thematically linked literary heritage poems from the WJEC poetry collection.

GCSE English Unit 3 Section A

For Unit 3 Section A you will be required to produce two pieces of work. The first of the two tasks will require you to produce a written assignment linking a play by Shakespeare with a group of thematically linked literary heritage poems from the WJEC poetry collection.

1.3.1 Literary Heritage Poetry

There are over sixty 'literary heritage' poems in the WJEC's poetry collection, but obviously you will not have to write about most of them. However, the more you read the poems, the more confident you will become in your understanding of particular poems and of poetry in general.

This chapter encourages you to read the poems freely, firstly by browsing and then by looking more closely at a range of poems.

Openings

Here are the openings to several of the poems in the WJEC collection. It is important when you read a poem that you 'position' yourself with the situation and the voice at the start of the poem.

The Passionate Shepherd to His Love

Christopher Marlowe

Come live with me and be my love,
And we will all the pleasures prove
That valleys, groves, hills, and fields,
Woods, or steepy mountain yields.

In the first example, above, you know from the title who is speaking to whom. You guess that the voice is passionate and that the situation is that the shepherd is asking his lover to live with him.

Dulce et Decorum Est
Wilfred Owen

Bent double, like old beggars under sacks,
Knock-kneed, coughing like hags, we cursed through sludge,
Till on the haunting flares we turned our backs
And towards our distant rest began to trudge.

Describe the situation as experienced by the poet at the start of 'Dulce et Decorum Est'. How can you tell the poet is present in the scene?

The Soldier
Rupert Brooke

If I should die, think only this of me:
That there's some corner of a foreign field
That is for ever England.

What do you think the situation is at the start of 'The Soldier'?

Song: The Willing Mistriss
Aphra Behn

Amyntas led me to a Grove,
Where all the Trees did shade us;
The Sun it self, though it had Strove,
It could not have betray'd us:

Explain the secrecy of the opening lines of 'The Willing Mistriss'.

My Heart is Like a Withered Nut!

Caroline Norton

My heart is like a withered nut,
Rattling within its hollow shell;
You cannot ope my breast, and put
Any thing fresh with it to dwell.

> **Describe the mood and attitude of the speaker in 'My Heart is Like a Withered Nut!'.**

Havisham

Carol Ann Duffy

Beloved sweetheart bastard. Not a day since then
I haven't wished him dead. Prayed for it
so hard I've dark green pebbles for eyes,
ropes on the back of my hands I could strangle with.

> **Describe the voice and situation of the speaker in 'Havisham'.**

Sonnet 18

William Shakespeare

Shall I compare thee to a summer's day?
Thou art more lovely and more temperate;

> **Who is the speaker addressing and what is the message in 'Sonnet 18'?**

Do not go gentle into that good night

Dylan Thomas

Do not go gentle into that good night,
Old age should burn and rave at close of day;
Rage, rage against the dying of the light.

> **Who is the speaker addressing and what is the message in 'Do not go gentle...'?**

Porphyria's Lover

Robert Browning

The rain set early in to-night,
The sullen wind was soon awake,
It tore the elm-tops down for spite,
And did its worst to vex the lake:
I listened with heart fit to break.

> **What is the mood of the speaker and the atmosphere of the opening to 'Porphyria's Lover'?**

Refugee Blues
WH Auden

Say this city has ten million souls,
Some are living in mansions, some are living in holes:
Yet there's no place for us, my dear, yet there's no place for us.

Who do you think the speaker is at the start of 'Refugee Blues'? To whom is he speaking? What is the situation?

Drummer Hodge
Thomas Hardy

They throw in Drummer Hodge, to rest
Uncoffined — just as found:
His landmark is a kopje-crest
That breaks the veldt around:
And foreign constellations west
Each night above his mound.

What is the situation being described by the poet-narrator at the start of 'Drummer Hodge'?

What is literary heritage poetry?

Literary heritage poetry links our present day to the past, and contributes to our understanding of history. The themes that run through the WJEC's collection of poems are as relevant now as ever.

POSSIBLE THEMES:
hypocrisy and prejudice, youth and age

In Church

Thomas Hardy

"And now to God the Father," he ends,
And his voice thrills up to the topmost tiles:
Each listener chokes as he bows and bends,
And emotion pervades the crowded aisles.
5 Then the preacher glides to the vestry-door,
And shuts it, and thinks he is seen no more.

What do you learn about the preacher in the first six lines?

The door swings softly ajar meanwhile,
And a pupil of his in the Bible class,
Who adores him as one without gloss or guile,
10 Sees her idol stand with a satisfied smile
And re-enact at the vestry-glass
Each pulpit gesture in deft dumb-show
That had moved the congregation so.

How does the preacher behave now? What is going through the mind of his pupil?

'In Church' by Thomas Hardy describes a preacher as viewed in public performance, and then by chance in private by a young admirer. How does Hardy present the character of the preacher?

A Woman to her Lover
Christina Walsh

POSSIBLE THEMES:
love, male-female relationships and the role of women

Do you come to me to bend me to your will
As conqueror to the vanquished
To make of me a bondslave
To bear you children, wearing out my life
5　In drudgery and silence
No servant will I be
If that be what you ask. O Lover I refuse you!

Or if you think to wed with one from heaven sent
whose every deed and word and wish is golden
10　a wingless angel who can do no wrong
go! – I am no doll to dress and sit for feeble worship
if that be what you ask, fool, I refuse you!

Or if you think in me to find
A creature who will have no greater joy
15　Than gratify your clamorous desire,
My skin soft only for your fond caresses
My body supple only for your sense delight.
Oh shame, and pity and abasement.
Not for you the hand of any wakened woman of our time.

20　But Lover, if you ask of me
That I shall be your comrade, friend, and mate,
To live and work, to love and die with you,
That so together we may know the purity and height
Of passion, and of joy and sorrow,
25　Then O husband, I am yours forever
And our co-equal love will make the stars to laugh with joy
And to its circling fugue pass on, hand holding hand
Until we reach the very heart of God.

What do you learn about the woman's attitude in these lines?

What details from the text make this clear?

What ideas does the poet want us to think about?

How does the woman change in these lines?

A woman addresses a man in 'A Woman to her Lover'. How does the poet present the woman's character and attitude in this poem?

The Sun Rising

John Donne

POSSIBLE THEMES:
love, male-female relationships

Busy old fool, unruly sun,
Why dost thou thus,
Through windows, and through curtains call on us?
Must to thy motions lovers' seasons run?
5 Saucy pedantic wretch, go chide
Late school-boys, and sour prentices,
Go tell court-huntsmen that the King will ride,
Call country ants to harvest offices;
Love, all alike, no season knows, nor clime,
10 Nor hours, days, months, which are the rags of time.

Thy beams, so reverend, and strong
Why shouldst thou think?
I could eclipse and cloud them with a wink,
But that I would not lose her sight so long:
15 If her eyes have not blinded thine,
Look, and to-morrow late tell, me,
Whether both the Indias of spice and mine
Be where thou left'st them, or lie here with me.
Ask for those kings whom thou saw'st yesterday,
20 And thou shalt hear, All here in one bed lay.

She's all states, and all princes I,
Nothing else is.
Princes do but play us; compared to this,
All honour's mimic, all wealth alchemy.
25 Thou sun art half as happy as we,
In that the world's contracted thus;
Thine age asks ease, and since thy duties be
To warm the world, that's done in warming us.
Shine here to us, and thou art everywhere;
30 This bed thy centre is, these walls, thy sphere.

What is the mood of the speaker at the start of the poem?

What details from the text make this clear?

What are the speaker's thoughts and feelings in the first two stanzas of the poem?

Write about the poet's choice of words.

How does the speaker praise his lover in this last stanza?

What does he say in the final two lines? What do you think of this as an ending?

In 'The Sun Rising', the sun invades the privacy of the lovers at the start of a new day. The speaker uses the occasion to pay tribute to his love. How does this persona describe and celebrate his love?

How do I love thee? Elizabeth Barrett Browning

POSSIBLE THEMES: love, male-female relationships

How do I love thee? Let me count the ways.
I love thee to the depth and breadth and height
My soul can reach, when feeling out of sight
For the ends of Being and ideal Grace.
5   I love thee to the level of every day's
Most quiet need, by sun and candlelight.
I love thee freely, as men strive for Right.
I love thee purely, as they turn from Praise.
I love thee with the passion put to use
10 In my old griefs, and with my childhood's faith.
I love thee with a love I seemed to lose
With my lost saints – I love thee with the breath,
Smiles, tears, of all my life! – and, if God choose,
I shall but love thee better after death.

What are your thoughts and feelings about the speaker and the 'voice' she uses? Use details from the text to support your points.

How effective is the ending of the poem?

In 'How do I love thee'? the speaker declares her love. How does she explain the full extent of her devotion to her lover?

Crabbed Age and Youth William Shakespeare

POSSIBLE THEMES: youth and age, conflict, hypocrisy and prejudice

Crabbed Age and Youth
Cannot live together:
Youth is full of pleasance,
Age is full of care;
5   Youth like summer morn,
Age like winter weather;
Youth like summer brave,
Age like winter bare:
Youth is full of sport,
10 Age's breath is short;
Youth is nimble, Age is lame:
Youth is hot and bold,
Age is weak and cold;
Youth is wild, and Age is tame:—
15 Age, I do abhor thee,
Youth, I do adore thee.
O! my love, my love is young!
Age, I do defy thee—
O sweet shepherd, hie thee,
20 For methinks thou stay'st too long.

What are your thoughts and feelings about the way the poem is organized and structured?

What impressions does the poet create of 'youth'?

What impressions does the poet create of 'age'?

Shakespeare speaks about 'Crabbed Age and Youth' in his poem of the same name. How does he present them?

On My First Son

Ben Jonson

Farewell, thou child of my right hand, and joy!
My sin was too much hope of thee, loved boy.
Seven years thou wert lent to me, and I thee pay,
Exacted by thy fate, on the just day.

5   Oh, could I lose all father now! For why
Will man lament the state he should envy—
To have so soon 'scaped world's and flesh's rage,
And, if no other misery, yet age?
Rest in soft peace, and, asked, say here doth lie

10 Ben Jonson his best piece of poetry:
For whose sake, henceforth, all his vows be such
As what he loves may never like too much.

What feelings does the poet reveal in these lines?

What are your thoughts and feelings as you read this poem?

What do you think about this as an ending?

In 'On My First Son', Ben Jonson speaks about the death of his young child. How does he present his tribute to his son?

The Send-Off

Wilfred Owen

POSSIBLE THEMES:
conflict, grief

Down the close darkening lanes they sang their way
To the siding-shed,
And lined the train with faces grimly gay.

Describe the scene in the first ten lines of the poem.

Their breasts were stuck all white with wreath and spray
5 As men's are, dead.

Comment on some of the poet's choice of words.

Dull porters watched them, and a casual tramp
Stood staring hard,
Sorry to miss them from the upland camp.

> 'The Send-Off' describes the departure of a train-load of soldiers for the front line in France and Belgium. How does the poet present the grim reality of the occasion?

Then, unmoved, signals nodded, and a lamp
10 Winked to the guard.

So secretly, like wrongs hushed-up, they went.
They were not ours:
We never heard to which front these were sent.

What are your thoughts and feelings about the second half of the poem?

Nor there if they yet mock what women meant
15 Who gave them flowers.

Shall they return to beating of great bells
In wild train-loads?
A few, a few, too few for drums and yells,

What happens in these lines?

What point is the poet trying to make here?

May creep back, silent, to village wells,
20 Up half-known roads.

Base Details

Siegfried Sassoon

If I were fierce, and bald, and short of breath,
I'd live with scarlet Majors at the Base,
And speed glum heroes up the line to death.
You'd see me with my puffy petulant face,
5 Guzzling and gulping in the best hotel,
Reading the Roll of Honour. 'Poor young chap,'
I'd say – 'I used to know his father well;
Yes, we've lost heavily in this last scrap.'
And when the war is done and youth stone dead,
10 I'd toddle safely home and die – in bed.

How does the poet present the high-ranking officers in this short poem?

Consider: their appearances, how they speak, how they behave.

'Base Details' is a satirical poem that comments bitterly on the role of the senior officers in the army during the war. How does the poet reveal his anger?

Leisure

WH Davies

POSSIBLE THEMES:
conflict, power and ambition

What is this life if, full of care,
We have no time to stand and stare?

No time to stand beneath the boughs
And stare as long as sheep and cows.

5 No time to see, when woods we pass,
Where squirrels hide their nuts in grass.

No time to see, in broad daylight,
Streams full of stars, like skies at night.

No time to turn at Beauty's glance,
10 And watch her feet, how they can dance.

No time to wait till her mouth can
Enrich that smile her eyes began.

A poor life this if, full of care,
We have no time to stand and stare.

Explain in your own words what the poet is trying to say about life.

What details in the poem are particularly effective in your opinion and why?

What does the poet finally say about life?

In 'Leisure', the poet complains about the pace of 20th-century life. How does he make us question our attitude to life and leisure?

Hawk Roosting

Ted Hughes

POSSIBLE THEMES: *power and ambition, conflict*

I sit in the top of the wood, my eyes closed.
Inaction, no falsifying dream
Between my hooked head and hooked feet:
Or in sleep rehearse perfect kills and eat.

5 The convenience of the high trees!
The air's buoyancy and the sun's ray
Are of advantage to me;
And the earth's face upward for my inspection.

My feet are locked upon the rough bark.
10 It took the whole of Creation
To produce my foot, my each feather:
Now I hold Creation in my foot

Or fly up, and revolve it all slowly –
I kill where I please because it is all mine.
15 There is no sophistry in my body:
My manners are tearing off heads –

The allotment of death.
For the one path of my flight is direct
Through the bones of the living.
20 No arguments assert my right:

The sun is behind me.
Nothing has changed since I began.
My eye has permitted no change.
I am going to keep things like this.

What do you think is going through the hawk's mind?

What impressions do you have of the hawk in these lines?

What ideas may the poet want us to think about by the end of this poem?

Use words and phrases from the poem to support your points.

In 'Hawk Roosting', the hawk looks down from the heights upon the world below. How does the poet portray the character of the hawk?

Follower

Seamus Heaney

POSSIBLE THEMES: *family and parent-child relationships, youth and age*

My father worked with a horse-plough,
His shoulders globed like a full sail strung
Between the shafts and the furrow.
The horse strained at his clicking tongue.

5   An expert. He would set the wing
And fit the bright steel-pointed sock.
The sod rolled over without breaking.
At the headrig, with a single pluck

Of reins, the sweating team turned round
10   And back into the land. His eye
Narrowed and angled at the ground,
Mapping the furrow exactly.

I stumbled in his hob-nailed wake,
Fell sometimes on the polished sod;
15   Sometimes he rode me on his back,
Dipping and rising to his plod.

I wanted to grow up and plough,
To close one eye, stiffen my arm.
All I ever did was follow
20   In his broad shadow round the farm.

I was a nuisance, tripping, falling,
Yapping always. But today
It is my father who keeps stumbling
Behind me, and will not go away.

What are your thoughts and feelings about the relationship between the poet and his father? Use details from the poem to support your points.

In the last two stanzas, how does the poet show that his relationship with his father has changed?

In 'Follower', Seamus Heaney looks back at his childhood. How does he present his relationship with his father?

Valentine

Carol Ann Duffy

POSSIBLE THEMES:
love, conflict

Not a red rose or a satin heart.

I give you an onion.
It is a moon wrapped in brown paper.
It promises light
5 like the careful undressing of love.

Here.
It will blind you with tears
like a lover.
It will make your reflection
10 a wobbling photo of grief.

I am trying to be truthful.

Not a cute card or a kissogram.

I give you an onion.
Its fierce kiss will stay on your lips,
15 possessive and faithful
as we are,
for as long as we are.

Take it.
Its platinum loops shrink to a wedding-ring,
20 if you like.
Lethal.
Its scent will cling to your fingers,
cling to your knife.

What are your thoughts and feelings about the first few lines of 'Valentine'?

What do you learn about the persona's attitude in these lines? Comment on the words and phrases used by the poet.

How effective is the ending of the poem? What ideas does the poet perhaps want us to think about?

'Valentine' by Carol Ann Duffy is a very un-romantic poem. How does the speaker in the poem make her beliefs apparent to her partner?

Long Distance II

Tony Harrison

POSSIBLE THEMES:
family and parent-child relationships, grief

Though my mother was already two years dead
Dad kept her slippers warming by the gas,
put hot water bottles her side of the bed
and still went to renew her transport pass.

What do you learn about the father and son and their relationship in these lines?

5   You couldn't just drop in. You had to phone.
He'd put you off an hour to give him time
to clear away her things and look alone
as though his still raw love were such a crime.

He couldn't risk my blight of disbelief
10   though sure that very soon he'd hear her key
scrape in the rusted lock and end his grief.
He knew she'd just popped out to get the tea.

What is going through the son's mind in the last eight lines of the poem?

I believe life ends with death, and that is all.
You haven't both gone shopping; just the same,
15   in my new black leather phone book there's your name
and the disconnected number I still call.

What are your thoughts and feelings about the ending of the poem?

> In 'Long Distance II', Tony Harrison reflects on the death of his mother and then the death of his father. How does he present attitudes to death in this poem?

Prayer Before Birth

Louis MacNeice

POSSIBLE THEMES:
power and ambition, family and parent-child relationships

I am not yet born; O hear me.
Let not the bloodsucking bat or the rat or the stoat or the
    club-footed ghoul come near me.

What thoughts do the first lines of the poem provoke in the reader?

I am not yet born, console me.
5   I fear that the human race may with tall walls wall me,
    with strong drugs dope me, with wise lies lure me,
      on black racks rack me, in blood-baths roll me.

I am not yet born; provide me
With water to dandle me, grass to grow for me, trees to talk
10   to me, sky to sing to me, birds and a white light
in the back of my mind to guide me.

I am not yet born; forgive me
For the sins that in me the world shall commit, my words
when they speak me, my thoughts when they think me,
15   my treason engendered by traitors beyond me,
my life when they murder by means of my
hands, my death when they live me.

I am not yet born; rehearse me
In the parts I must play and the cues I must take when
20   old men lecture me, bureaucrats hector me, mountains
frown at me, lovers laugh at me, the white
waves call me to folly and the desert calls
me to doom and the beggar refuses
my gift and my children curse me.

25 I am not yet born; O hear me,
Let not the man who is beast or who thinks he is God
come near me.

I am not yet born; O fill me
With strength against those who would freeze my
30   humanity, would dragoon me into a lethal automaton,
would make me a cog in a machine, a thing with
one face, a thing, and against all those
who would dissipate my entirety, would
blow me like thistledown hither and
35   thither or hither and thither
like water held in the
hands would spill me.

Let them not make me a stone and let them not spill me.
Otherwise kill me.

What is the poet saying about the life and the world that the unborn child will face? Support your points with words and phrases from the poem.

What do these lines add to the poem?

How effective is the ending of the poem?

In 'Prayer Before Birth', Louis MacNeice imagines the thoughts of an unborn child. How does he present the hopes and the fears of the child?

Studying poetry

Students are often very uncertain about studying poetry. So, bear the following points in mind as you begin to read more of it:

- You need to build up your confidence with poetry. Do not worry too much about technical language. Learn to read a poem properly by approaching it sentence by sentence.
- You may not be able to read a poem out loud (in an examination, for example!), but you should try to at least hear the words of the poem in your head as you read.
- See a poem as a piece of drama or a narrative. Just like plays and novels, poems can have characters and stories. Poems may involve people, places, events, and have twisting plots. Even the shortest poem can have a beginning, a middle, and an end – in other words, poems have development, moving forward rather than standing still.
- Identify the speaking voice (or voices) in any poem that you read.
- Work out the situation at the start of any poem that you read.
- Do not always look to your teacher for the 'right' answer; there is often no absolute 'right' answer where poetry is concerned.

Unlocking the meaning of a poem

Each poem will generate its own unique questions to help you understand it, but here is a set of questions that you might ask yourself about any poem.

- What is the content of the poem – what is it about? (For example, is there a 'story'? Are there any characters? Who are they? What is their relationship? What is their background?)
- From whose viewpoint are we seeing the poem? The poet's? A character's? How does this affect our reading of the poem?
- What kind of mood or atmosphere does the poet want to create?
- How does the style contribute to your understanding of the poem? How is it written? What words or phrases do you find interesting? How are they organized?
- What ideas does the poet want to share with you? What are the themes of the poem and how do they develop?
- What is your response to the poem?

Technical matters

You can talk and write about poetry perfectly well without knowing many technical terms. Sometimes, technical language actually gets in the way of what you are trying to say about a poem's meaning. However, sensible use of terminology is a good thing and no one should feel it is beyond them. Increase your technical vocabulary gradually and use it in your writing only where it is relevant to the points you are trying to make.

Use some of the questions below when talking or writing about poems:

Choice of words and phrases
1. Which words and phrases stand out as particularly important?
2. Which are especially effective or surprising?
3. What are the subtle, suggestive meanings?

4.   Which words have a strong impact?

5.   What images are created by descriptive vocabulary, similes, and metaphors?

6.   Do any words involve the senses?

7.   Does the vocabulary evoke a mood or atmosphere in the poem?

8.   Does the vocabulary create tension or contrasts in the poem?

Sentences, word order, punctuation, and line-arrangements

1.   Are there grammatical patterns and features that stand out in the poem? How do they contribute to the meaning of the poem?

2.   Are there repetitions, line divisions, or features of punctuation that clarify or confuse the meaning?

3.   How complex or simple is the language at different points in the poem?

4.   Are there any sound patterns worthy of comment – onomatopoeia, alliteration, assonance, rhythms, rhymes, and stresses?

5.   Does the overall shape or structure of the poem add to your understanding of it?

6.   How does the whole poem relate to its title or vice-versa?

7.   How does the whole poem relate to the voice and the setting at the start of the poem?

EXAMINER'S TIP

Do this…

- Always try to make comments that show your understanding of the poem.
- Use the technical terms only if they fit the poem that you are working on, and only if you have a sensible comment to make on the features you have spotted.

Don't do this…

- 'This poem contains lots of similes and metaphors. It has an ABABCDCD rhyme scheme… It has six stanzas with four lines in each stanza… There are ten syllables in each line…' etc.

Biographical details and cultural contexts

Relevant facts about a poet's life are known as **biographical details**. The **cultural context** of a poem refers to the historical period or periods that relate to it and also the place in which the poet lived, and the influence these had on the poem.

- Adding this information to your essay needs to be planned carefully, so the reader knows why you are telling them these facts – i.e. what they add to your understanding of the poem.
- Weave your comments about the poet and the historical period into your writing – don't just bolt them on to the beginning or the end of your essay.
- Do not pad out your essay with biographical details or information about the cultural context of the poet directly from the Internet. Some students mistakenly write pages about the poet and virtually nothing to show they have understood the poems.

Linking different aspects of poems

You can link any of the following aspects, but be selective and thoughtful. Choose the aspects that you can develop a little. Don't limit yourself to spotting and listing!

- **Theme**
  What aspect of the theme is being considered?
- **Personal response**
  Do you think the poet succeeded in doing what he/she set out to do?
- **Mood**
  What kind of mood does the poet try to create? Does it change?
- **Viewpoint**
  Is the poem personal or objective? Does the poet view the characters and emotions from a distance or is he/she 'in' the poem and experiencing them?
- **Narrative**
  What kind of 'story' does the poet set his/her theme in?
- **Setting**
  Where is the poem set? Is the setting important?
- **Type**
  Is the poem a lyric, a narrative, a ballad, a dramatic poem, or a descriptive poem?
- **Structure**
  How is the poem put together? Is it a series of argument, a story? Is it written in parts? If so, how do they relate to each other?
- **Style**
  What kind of images does the poet use? Is the language highly figurative (lots of metaphors and similes)? Does the poet use irony? Are there any unexpected twists in the poem? Is the style conversational, complex, formal, or colloquial?
- **Period**
  When was the poem written? Does the date suggest that there may have been different attitudes when the poem was written? Does this affect the style, imagery, and vocabulary?

1.3.2 Shakespeare

A Shakespeare play has five acts.

The play may be a tragedy like *Macbeth* or *Romeo & Juliet* with a dark ending, but even tragedies have comic moments too. Tragedies end with the inevitable, fateful deaths of major characters.

The play may be a comedy like *Twelfth Night* or *The Taming of the Shrew*, but comedies have dark moments too and can also deal with serious issues. For most characters Shakespearean comedies end with marriages and celebrations.

Like *The Tempest* and *The Merchant of Venice*, the play might be neither a comedy nor a tragedy, but include features of both. *Henry V* (celebrating a great English triumph) or *Julius Caesar* (exploring the chaos caused by overthrowing a leader) are both history plays; plays based on famous episodes in history.

Reading the text

Shakespeare was both a great dramatist and a great poet. You should try to experience the drama in the theatre or on the screen. When you read the text yourself, be bold and read for clarity, rhythm and meaning.

1. Pronounce individual words clearly and confidently.
2. Read slowly and deliberately, stressing key words and syllables.
3. Use the punctuation.
4. Ensue that you understand the difference between verse and prose in Shakespeare.

Read the famous speech in verse from *As You Like It*, known as 'The Seven Ages of Man' on page 78. In the speech, the punctuation has been deliberately enlarged and emboldened to emphasise the pauses. Read it aloud, following the advice above.

The Seven Ages of Man
William Shakespeare

All the world's a stage
And all the men and women merely players:
They have their exits and their entrances
And one man in his time plays many parts,

5 His acts being seven ages. At first the infant,
Mewling and puking in the nurse's arms;
Then the whining schoolboy with his satchel
And shining morning face, creeping like snail
Unwillingly to school; and then the lover,

10 Sighing like furnace, with a woeful ballad
Made to his mistress' eyebrow; then a soldier,
Full of strange oaths and bearded like the pard,
Jealous in honor, sudden, and quick in quarrel,
Seeking the bubble 'reputation'

15 Even in the cannon's mouth; and then the justice,
In fair round belly with good capon lin'd,
With eyes severe and beard of formal cut,
Full of wise saws and modern instances —
And so he plays his part; the sixth age shifts

20 Into the lean and slipper'd pantaloon,
With spectacles on nose and pouch on side,
His youthful hose well sav'd — a world too wide
For his shrunk shank — and his big manly voice,
Turning again toward childish treble, pipes

25 And whistles in his sound; last scene of all
That ends this strange eventful history
Is second childishness and mere oblivion,
Sans teeth, sans eyes, sans taste, sans everything.

Verse and prose

Shakespeare's plays are mainly written in verse. This is a convention, a 'rule' of the Elizabethan theatre. Verse is not how people spoke in reality! However, it acts as a distinction from prose, which also features in the plays - think of it like Standard English (verse) being different from dialect (prose), or formal English (verse) and informal English (prose).

The verse in Shakespeare's plays is largely unrhymed, though you will spot some rhyming, especially at the end of scenes and key speeches.

> **Scan the play you are studying for examples of rhyme.**

Verse within the world of the Shakespearean play is suitable for most occasions - from royalty down to high-ranking soldiers and officials, to characters that interact with them, such as servants who would have to speak 'proper' to their superiors. By playing with the rhythms of the verse and avoiding a monotonous beat, Shakespeare created individual 'voices' for his characters, representing a spectrum of moods and emotions.

Prose has its place in Shakespeare's plays too, extending the range of voices and the spectrum of social types even further. 'Lowlifes' would probably only speak prose (street-language), but potentially all of the other characters would be able to interchange between verse and prose, depending on to whom they were talking and why. Typically, speech or dialogue that is conspiratorial, very informal, disrespectful or casual is presented in prose.

You do not need to know about the technical aspects of verse, but it is very useful to know the broad differences between the verse and the prose in Shakespeare's plays.

> **Look through the play you are studying and identify when and why each of the characters speaks in verse and when and why they speak in prose.**

Entrances and exits

A reading 'performance' by a group or class (or even in the head of an individual student) needs to take account of the entrances and exits during the play. Who is coming and going? Who is present in a particular scene?

The problem with a seated class reading (or a private reading) is that the entrances and exits are sometimes lost, and the action and meaning of the play can also be lost as a result. A group or class really needs to observe the stage directions, especially to appreciate when a character is alone, or, as often happens in Shakespeare, alone in a crowd.

Note when people come and go. Note also when they think aloud in asides, which are private moments shared with the audience.

Look for the entrances, exits and asides in the play you are studying. Make a note particularly of occasions when a character delivers a long aside to an audience. This is a key feature of Shakespeare's plays: The confidential speech is known as a soliloquy.

Know your characters

List the characters in the play you are studying, in the order in which they appear. Make a grid similar to the one below, representing scene-by-scene appearances throughout the play. This will reinforce your awareness of the interaction of characters. Make a note of key exits, entrances and asides during scenes.

Character	Act 1	Act 2	Act 3	Act 4	Act 5

Know the plot

In very brief bullet-point form, make a list in sentences of the key twists and turns of the play you are studying. Make sure each scene is represented and make sure that each act is grouped separately. Do not write a long-hand version of the summary of the play as found in some study guides!

Themes and words

On pages 82 – 84 you will find a collection of some significant quotations and short passages from Shakespeare's plays.

Discuss each of the quotations, with one eye on the themes in the play that you are studying. Make a clear and considered comment on each of the quotations in writing.

A Thou wouldst be great,
Art not without ambition, but without
The illness should attend it. What thou wouldst highly,
That wouldst thou holily; wouldst not play false,
And yet wouldst wrongly win.

MACBETH

B The quality of mercy is not strain'd,
It droppeth as the gentle rain from heaven
Upon the place beneath. It is twice blest:
It blesseth him that gives, and him that takes.

THE MERCHANT OF VENICE

C Cowards die many times before their deaths,
The valiant never taste of death but once.

JULIUS CAESAR

D False face must hide what the false heart doth know.

MACBETH

E All that glisters is not gold;
Often have you heard that told.

THE MERCHANT OF VENICE

F The devil can cite Scripture for his purpose.

THE MERCHANT OF VENICE

G Every subject's duty is the king's, but every
subject's soul is his own.

HENRY V

H And oftentimes, to win us to our harm,
The instruments of darkness tell us truths;
Win us with honest trifles, to betray's
In deepest consequence—

MACBETH

I It is a wise father that knows his own child.

THE MERCHANT OF VENICE

J The evil that men do lives after them,
The good is oft interred with their bones.

JULIUS CAESAR

K How far that little candle throws his beams!
So shines a good deed in a naughty world.

THE MERCHANT OF VENICE

L ...be not afraid of greatness. Some are born great,
some achieve greatness, and some have greatness thrust upon 'em.

TWELFTH NIGHT

M What, man, ne'er pull your hat upon your brows:
Give sorrow words; the grief that does not speak,
Whispers the o'erfraught heart and bids it break.

MACBETH

N Will all great Neptune's ocean wash this blood
Clean from my hand?

MACBETH

O O, how bitter a thing it is to look into happiness through
    another man's eyes.

AS YOU LIKE IT

P I hate ingratitude more in a man
Than lying, vainness, babbling drunkenness,
Or any taint of vice whose strong corruption
Inhabits our frail blood.

TWELFTH NIGHT

Q Love sought is good, but given unsought is better.

TWELFTH NIGHT

R Love is blind, and lovers cannot see
The pretty follies that themselves commit.

THE MERCHANT OF VENICE

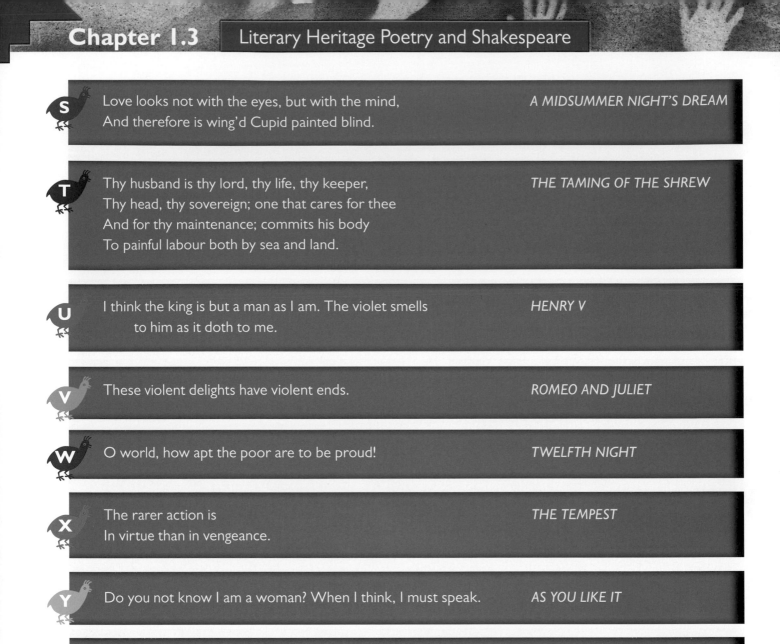

S

Love looks not with the eyes, but with the mind,
And therefore is wing'd Cupid painted blind.

A MIDSUMMER NIGHT'S DREAM

T

Thy husband is thy lord, thy life, thy keeper,
Thy head, thy sovereign; one that cares for thee
And for thy maintenance; commits his body
To painful labour both by sea and land.

THE TAMING OF THE SHREW

U

I think the king is but a man as I am. The violet smells
to him as it doth to me.

HENRY V

V

These violent delights have violent ends.

ROMEO AND JULIET

W

O world, how apt the poor are to be proud!

TWELFTH NIGHT

X

The rarer action is
In virtue than in vengeance.

THE TEMPEST

Y

Do you not know I am a woman? When I think, I must speak.

AS YOU LIKE IT

Z

A woman mov'd is like a fountain troubled,
Muddy, ill-seeming, thick, bereft of beauty.

THE TAMING OF THE SHREW

1.3.3 Linking literary heritage poetry and Shakespeare

In preparation for your Controlled Assessment task, you will have studied a Shakespeare play and the WJEC poetry collection. When you write your assignment under controlled conditions, you will need to draw upon your understanding of the whole Shakespeare play that you have studied as well as your reading of a range of poetry from the collection. The Shakespeare play and the poems that you write about will be linked by theme.

There are eight broad themes identified for the linked study. Two (or three) will be nominated by the exam board each year. For English Literature candidates, you cannot choose to study *Othello* or *Much Ado About Nothing* for this assessment, because these plays are an option for examination elsewhere on the course.

The themes are:
- love
- family and parent-child relationships
- youth and age
- power and ambition
- male-female relationships and the role of women
- hypocrisy and prejudice
- conflict
- grief.

This chapter has encouraged you to engage with the whole of the Shakespeare play you are studying and as much of the poetry collection as possible. This will add to your confidence in writing about the poems and the parts of the play you will eventually choose to focus on. Your teacher may choose to begin with the Shakespeare or with some of the poems. Every single Shakespeare play broadly covers the themes and most of the poems cover more than one of the themes. Initially, get to know the plot and the characters of your Shakespeare play, and get to know what the poems are about. Don't worry at the reading stage of the process about the themes and the links! Enjoy the drama and the verse.

Controlled Assessment Practice

Example generic task:

1. Many plays and poems are concerned with the relationship between men and women. Choose one relationship between a man and a woman in the drama you have studied and link it with a similar relationship in the poetry you have studied.

Examples of specific tasks:

2. • How does Shakespeare portray the role of women in *The Taming of the Shrew* throughout the play?
   • The role of women is also presented in a number of the poems you have studied. Discuss the way the role of the women is portrayed in the poetry you have studied.
   • What is your personal response to the literature you have studied? In your answer you must explore the links between the poetry and the Shakespeare play.

3. • Look at the way Shakespeare presents Katherine's relationship with Petruchio in *The Taming of the Shrew* throughout the play. Consider what Petruchio says about how women should behave and Katherine's reaction to his views.
   • Consider the way the role of women is presented in poems in the collection. Write about one poem in particular but make references to others.
   • What is your personal response to the literature you have studied? In your answer you must explore the links between the poetry and the Shakespeare play you have studied.

Extracts from sample answers

Both of the following extracts are from essays on the theme of love. The first examines *Hamlet* in relation to love and the second looks at the poetry of John Donne.

Student response Question 1 extract 1

...During his recollections Hamlet also displays his disgust at his mother. It sounds as if she was merely using her husband, instead of loving him. Maybe Hamlet's view of his mother has become so tarnished because her actions have coloured what would otherwise have been happy memories.

Certainly this feeling is strengthened in the way he declares 'frailty, thy name is woman'. Just like Hamlet's view of the world has become distorted and muddied by his grief for his father, his perception of women has been ruined by the actions of his mother.

Hamlet continues to consider recent events, especially the remarriage of his mother. He complains how 'a little month' after she was mourning at her husband's funeral she married his brother. There are constant references to this such as:

'Ere yet the salt of most unrighteous tears
Had left the flushing in her galled eyes,
She married.'

The phrase 'She married' is tacked on to the end of the sentence, which gives it an added tone of disbelief. This quote also displays how Hamlet's opinion of his mother had deteriorated. He believes that she cried 'unrighteous tears', and earlier likens her to 'a beast that wants discourse of reason'.

EXAMINER'S COMMENT

The student discusses the character of Hamlet clearly, and has some strong views and makes some more careful observations. In the extract there are short quotations integrated into the writing and there is one longer quotation, which is fully backed up with comments. The student writes in detail about his mother and her re-marriage.

Student response Question 1 extract 2

I like John Donne's poetry because no way can you say it is gushy and sentimental, and you cannot say that about Hamlet either. Shakespeare and Donne wrote during the same period of history and it was a tough world. There was a lot of passion for loving and fighting, and you could easily see how Hamlet could be the speaker in a poem like 'Since she whom I lov'd'. Love is a complex and uncertain matter for Hamlet and he is also at odds with himself and everyone else...

EXAMINER'S COMMENT

This student has already begun to prove his or her quality when writing about the poetry and the play and sets off comfortably linking the two. The confidence shines through with personal responses merged with historical awareness: A strong opening.

How is Unit 3 assessed at GCSE?

Reading and understanding texts: is there...

- ❑ a reasonably even attempt to respond to the play identifying some basic links?
- ❑ some relevant detailed response to both play and poems, with some personal response and some cross-references?
- ❑ a detailed understanding of the relevant theme as covered by both play and poems?
- ❑ a well-reasoned and thorough understanding of the relevant theme as covered in both play and poems?

Writer's ideas: is there...

- ❑ some response to characters, relationships and main events?
- ❑ some detail to back-up views and some basic awareness of the writers' use of language?
- ❑ evidence of a clearly expressed personal response supported by well-chosen references to aspects of language and structure?
- ❑ a confident analysis and interpretation of characters and language?

Expression and organization: does the finished essay show...

- ❑ a response to both texts in relation to the theme with a personal response linking the texts?
- ❑ a fairly well-balanced response to the different parts of the task?
- ❑ a focused response to the question and the theme throughout?
- ❑ a precise, succinct response that is a thorough exploration of the ways the writers have dealt with the theme?

Preparing for Controlled Assessment

Here are the relevant details from the GCSE specification for this part of the assessment, including the relevant Assessment Objectives for the English Literature and English specifications.

GCSE ENGLISH LITERATURE UNIT 3: Poetry and drama (literary heritage)

Controlled Assessment

English/Irish/Welsh literary heritage: Poetry and Shakespeare play (25%)
You will need to write **one** task linking the study of a play by Shakespeare to poetry from the WJEC collection.

AO1

- Respond to texts critically and imaginatively; select and evaluate relevant textual detail to illustrate and support interpretations.

AO2

- Explain how language, structure and form contribute to writers' presentation of ideas, themes and settings.

AO3

- Make comparisons and explain links between texts, evaluating writers' different ways of expressing meaning and achieving effects.

 GCSE ENGLISH UNIT 3: English in the world of the imagination; different cultures prose

Reading: literary texts: literary heritage poetry & Shakespeare (10%)

Controlled Assement

You will need to write **one** task linking the study of a play by Shakespeare to poetry from the WJEC collection.

AO2 Reading

- Read and understand texts, selecting material appropriate to purpose, collating from different sources and making comparisons and cross-references as appropriate.
- Develop and sustain interpretations of writers' ideas and perspectives.
- Explain and evaluate how writers use linguistic, grammatical, structural and presentational features to achieve effects and engage and influence the reader.
- Understand texts in their social, cultural and historical contexts.

The Writing Process

Will I have time in class to prepare my essay?

Yes, after initially reading the texts, you will have up to 15 hours of lesson time to make suitable notes on your texts and to plan your approach.

Can I have help from the teacher?

Your teacher can help you in the normal way - by teaching the class and talking to you individually. However, you are not allowed to obtain help from your teacher during your revision.

How long is the Controlled Assessment?

For the linked essay, the Controlled Assessment time is **four hours**. This will probably be broken into shorter sessions so your teacher will collect your work after each session.

What are the rules for taking notes and copies of the texts into the Controlled Assessment?

You are allowed to take in one A4 sheet of **your own** notes. Clean copies of the texts are allowed. (If you do not have clean copies of texts to use, this will be noted in the information to the WJEC moderator, so that it is taken into account.)

How will the essay be marked?

Your work on the play and the poems will be marked out of 40 as one complete essay.

Chapter 1.4

Prose from different cultures is assessed differently in the English Literature and English specifications.

● For English Literature, it is assessed in a written exam.
● For English, it is assessed through a Controlled Assessment task.

FOCUS ON THE EXAM   **L1 UNIT 1**

GCSE English Literature Unit 1 Section A

In Section A of the exam, you will be asked to answer two questions on a prose text from a different culture. The first question (part (a)) will require close reading of an extract. The second question will provide a choice of tasks (parts (b) and (c)) relating to the whole text.

FOCUS ON CONTROLLED ASSESSMENT   **E UNIT 3**

GCSE English Unit 3 Section A

For Unit 3 Section A, you will be required to produce two pieces of work. The second will be a study of a prose text from a different culture.

What makes 'different cultures' different?

The world is a landscape of different languages, skin colours, and communities. Literature from different cultures allows us to see how the wider world works. As novels generally deal with human dilemmas, novels from different cultures let us see the problems that people face in various places throughout the world, not all of them far from home.

When you study your chosen text, you will explore how it reflects and influences people's values and assumptions of their own culture. Importantly, though, you will also see the close similarities in the hopes and dreams people have around the world, both in our own society and in 'different cultures'.

In these texts:
- you might witness a world of harshness and struggle
- you might be shocked by prejudice and injustice
- you might admire how people cope with the experience of racism
- you might marvel how they stand up to the tragedy of uncontrollable events
- you might even smile at someone caught between two cultures.

> **List the features of the novel that you are studying that make it a 'different cultures' novel. Range from large differences to small details.**

Openings

The opening of a novel tries to make a reader curious. It sometimes plunges you straight into the action. Sometimes it will start quietly by setting the scene or even by looking back, giving hints of what is to come.

When looking at openings, some of the questions you may want to ask yourself are:
- How does the story start?
- What is the first paragraph or page made-up of?
- How are you drawn into the story?
- What holds your attention?
- How much does the writer tell you?
- Is it possible to tell how the story will develop?

> **Read the extract below. What can you work out from the first lines of this novel?**

Chanda's Secrets

I'm alone in the office of Bateman's Eternal Light Funeral Services. It's early Monday morning and Mr Bateman is busy with a new shipment of coffins.

'I'll get to you as soon as I can,' he told me. 'Meanwhile, you can go into my office and look at my fish. They're in an aquarium on the far wall. If you get bored, there're magazines on the coffee table. By the way, I'm sorry about your sister.'

I don't want to look at Mr Bateman's fish. And I certainly don't want to read. I just want to get this meeting over with before I cry and make a fool of myself.

> **Look at the opening page of the novel that you are studying in this section and list what you learn about what is to come.**

The reader's response

The way that a reader responds to what a writer writes will vary according to each individual. The reader is likely to have a mixture of thoughts and feelings towards a character or a situation. He or she may be puzzled by what is happening or may be involved emotionally, or often both. Any personal response is a mixture of head and heart.

> **Read the passage from *Of Mice and Men* below. What are your thoughts and feelings about what happens in this extract?**

Of Mice and Men

Only Lennie was in the barn, and Lennie sat in the hay beside a packing case under a manger in the end of the barn that had not been filled with hay. Lennie sat in the hay and looked at a little dead puppy that lay in front of him. Lennie looked at it for a long time, and then he put out his huge hand and stroked it clear from one end to the other.

And Lennie said softly to the puppy, "Why do you got to get killed? You ain't so little as mice. I didn't bounce you hard." He bent the pup's head up and looked in its face, and he said to it, "Now maybe George ain't gonna let me tend no rabbits, if he fin's out you got killed."

He scooped a little hollow and laid the puppy in it and covered it over with hay, out of sight; but he continued to stare at the mound he had made. He said, "This ain't no bad thing like I got to go hide in the brush. Oh! No. This ain't. I'll tell George I foun' it dead."

He unburied the puppy and inspected it, and he stroked it from ears to tail. He went on sorrowfully, "But he'll know. George always knows. He'll say, 'You done it. Don't try to put nothing over on me.' An' he'll say, 'Now jus' for that you don't get to tend no rabbits!'

Suddenly his anger arose. "God damn you," he cried. "Why do you got to get killed? You ain't so little as mice." He picked up the pup and hurled it from him. He turned his back on it. He sat bent over his knees and he whispered, "Now I won't get to tend the rabbits. Now he won't let me." He rocked himself back and forth in his sorrow.

Choose an extract from the novel you are studying where a character is alone. With detailed reference to the extract, write down your thoughts and feelings towards the character.

Suspense

Suspense is closely linked to tension, which is an atmosphere of nervousness and unease. Suspense is the build-up of tension to a climax, often maintained by a writer's skills of keeping the reader guessing for as long as possible. The height of the tension is likely to be a memorable key scene in the novel. When the suspense is ended, the moments that follow also add to the drama.

Look at the following extract from *To Kill Mockingbird*. How does the author make the scene tense and dramatic?

To Kill a Mockingbird

[...] Mr Tate said, 'This court will come to order,' in a voice that rang with authority, and the heads below us jerked up. Mr Tate left the room and returned with Tom Robinson. He steered Tom to his place beside Atticus, and stood there. Judge Taylor had roused himself to sudden alertness and was sitting up straight looking at the empty jury box.

What happened after that had a dreamlike quality: in a dream I saw the jury return, moving like underwater swimmers, and Judge Taylor's voice came from far away, and was tiny...

[...] A jury never looks at a defendant it has convicted, and when this jury came in, not one of them looked at Tom Robinson. The foreman handed a piece of paper to Mr Tate who handed it to the clerk who handed it to the judge...

I shut my eyes. Judge Taylor was polling the jury: 'Guilty...guilty...guilty... guilty...' I peeked at Jem: his hands were white from gripping the balcony rail, and his shoulders jerked as if each 'guilty' was a separate stab between them.

Judge Taylor was saying something. His gavel was in his fist, but he wasn't using it. Dimly, I saw Atticus pushing papers from the table into his brief-case. He snapped it shut, went to the court reporter and said something, nodded to Mr Gilmer, and then went to Tom Robinson and whispered something to him. Atticus put his hand on Tom's shoulder as he whispered...

Choose an extract from the novel that you are studying where there is great suspense. Explore how the writer creates the dramatic build-up of excitement in those lines.

Humour

Humour is sometimes so personal that it is difficult to pinpoint what is funny or amusing about a text. However, unfamiliar situations do produce comic scenes and moments that make you smile, chuckle or even laugh out loud. Characters are sometimes put in a degree of discomfort by the writer, and the situation can strike a note of familiarity for the reader. Sometimes you might find yourself laughing at the character and sometimes you might be laughing with them. Humour occurs not just in books that advertise themselves as funny; it happens at the most unlikely moments in novels that have an overall serious intent.

> **The following scene from *Anita and Me* is humorous – why? Explain in detail what is amusing about it.**

Anita and Me

Mama had gone to the trouble of preparing two menus, which was fortunate considering Anita's reaction when the serving dishes of various curries were placed in front of her. 'What's that!' she demanded, as if confronted with a festering sheep's head on a platter. 'Oh that's mattar-paneer,' mama said proudly, always happy to educate the sad English palate. 'A sort of Indian cheese, and these are peas with it, of course...'

'Cheese and peas?' said Anita faintly. 'Together?'

'Well,' mama went on hurriedly 'This is chicken curry...You have had chicken before, haven't you?'

'What's that stuff round it?'

'Um, just gravy, you know, tomatoes, onions, garlic...'

Mama was losing confidence now, she trailed off as she picked up Anita's increasing panic.

'Chicken with tomatoes? What's garlic?'

'Don't you worry!' Papa interjected heartly, fearing a culinary cat fight was about to shatter his fragile peace. 'We've also got fishfingers and chips. Is tomato sauce too dangerous for you?'

Anita's relief made her oblivious to his attempt at a joke.

> **Choose an extract that contains some humour from the novel that you are studying and explain how the humour works.**

Mood and atmosphere

Atmosphere is very important when writing a novel. Think about the text you are studying. What is the mood and atmosphere like at the start of the story and how is the reader likely to react to this? How does the this change, if at all, during the story? What effect do the different settings or locations have on the mood and atmosphere?

Feelings

Most novels will contain at least one character that the reader will sympathize with. Often it is the character who tells the story, the narrator. The sympathy of the reader may come from a particular incident or from the essential goodness of the character.

> **How does the writer show the leading character's feelings in the extract below?**

I Know Why the Caged Bird Sings

I had a baby. He was beautiful and mine. Totally mine. No one had bought him for me. No one had helped me endure the sickly grey months. I had had help in the child's conception, but no one could deny that I had had an immaculate pregnancy.

Totally my possession, and I was afraid to touch him. Home from the hospital, I sat for hours by his bassinet and absorbed his mysterious perfection. His extremities were so dainty they appeared unfinished. Mother handled him easily with the casual confidence of a baby nurse, but I dreaded being forced to change his diapers. Wasn't I famous for awkwardness? Suppose I let him slip, or put my fingers on that throbbing pulse on the top of his head?

Mother came to my bed one night bringing my three-week old baby. She pulled the cover back and told me to get up while she put rubber sheets on my bed. She explained that he was going to sleep with me.

I begged in vain. I was sure to roll over and crush out his life or break those fragile bones. She wouldn't hear of it, and within minutes the pretty golden baby was lying on his back in the center of my bed, laughing at me.

> **Select an extract from the novel you are studying that expresses a character's private feelings and show in detail how the writer achieves it.**

The narrator is the storyteller of a novel or short story. There are two kinds of narrator: the one who stands outside the story as an observer and commentator (the **third-person narrator**); the other who is a character within the story (the **first-person narrator**). Every good novel and short story has a distinct narrative style. When the narrator actually has the 'voice' of a particular character, the viewpoint of the narrator will be restricted to the eyes and ears of that character.

How is Different Cultures Prose assessed at GCSE?

Does the response to the text...

❏ show some personal response to the text and general knowledge of the story?

❏ show some understanding of main features and selection of relevant detail?

❏ discuss characters and relationships thoughtfully, probe the sub-text, and select and evaluate relevant textual details?

❏ make assured selection and use of relevant detail, with thoughtful judgements on characters and relationships?

❏ consistently handle the text with confidence, with an overview and ability to move from the specific to the general?

Are there...

❏ generalized comments about language, structure and form?

❏ simple comments on particular features of style and structure?

❏ comments about how different aspects of style and structure create effects, meanings and ideas?

❏ assured comments exploring meaning and appreciating language and structure?

❏ assured and developed analytical comments on stylistic features?

Is there...

❏ a selection of simple comments on the background of the text?

❏ a limited awareness of social/cultural and historical contexts?

❏ a clear grasp of social/cultural and historical contexts?

❏ a range of clear comments on the importance of social/cultural and historical contexts?

❏ a clear selection of evidence from the text, which is used to support a clear understanding of social/cultural and historical contexts?

Is the expression (the grammar, punctuation and spelling)...

❏ likely to impede communication on occasions?

❏ reasonably clear with a basic structure, where errors are not too intrusive but specialist vocabulary is limited?

❏ mainly clear and fluent and quite well-structured, with only occasional errors in spelling or punctuation and specialist vocabulary used appropriately?

❏ clear and fluent and the answer well-structured, with few errors in grammar, punctuation and spelling and specialist vocabulary used appropriately?

Preparing for the exam

Here are the relevant details from the GCSE specification for this part of the assessment, including the relevant Assessment Objectives for the English Literature specification.

GCSE ENGLISH LITERATURE UNIT 1 Section A: Prose (different cultures)

Individual texts in context (21%)

Examination

You will answer **two** questions on a different cultures prose text. The first question will require close reading of an extract. The second question will offer a choice of tasks relating to the text as a whole.

AO1

● Respond to texts critically and imaginatively; select and evaluate relevant textual detail to illustrate and support interpretations.

AO2

● Explain how language, structure and form contribute to writers' presentation of ideas, themes and settings.

What is an essay?

An **essay** is a continuous piece of writing on a subject. In English Literature, you would not expect to see sub-headings or illustrations in an essay – therefore making **paragraphs** is an essential part of creating the structure.

Discursive writing in English Literature requires you to organize your own selection of facts and opinions to respond to a fairly open task or question. In fact, a discursive essay is a **one-way discussion**, so you have to work hard to keep to the question.

In a **closed book exam**, you show your knowledge and understanding of your set text by **direct quotation or referring to details of the text**.

Direct reference and detailed knowledge can be shown through **confident use of names, specific details, paraphrase** and **very short, embedded quotations** (usually a word or a phrase).

Writing your exam essay

- Divide your time wisely between each question on the paper. Read all of the questions quickly at the start of the exam. Let your subconscious mind do some work.
- Answer the question, which means do the task as set.
- Start at the sharp end; your first impressions are vital. Think before you start.
- Give the examiner something positive to tick in the first sentence.
- Make the examiner think, "high grade?" after the first paragraph.
- Get the writer in your essay early – see the writer as part of the discussion.
- Quotations should be short, frequent and integrated. The standard length of a quote should be the 'phrase' i.e. less than a full sentence. However, the 'single word' quote may be appropriate and so might a whole sentence occasionally.
- Echo (or refer back to) the question in every paragraph. Often, one word will do it. If none of your paragraph ties with the question, then you have drifted away. If so, don't panic, but return to the trail promptly.
- Get to the heart of the text or character at the start of the question. Have enthusiasm and respect for each text.
- Conveying a developed overview of each text should be a priority, however localized the extract you are working with. Don't leave the exam regretting missed opportunities to discuss key meanings of the texts – it's your chance. Make your essay work on the level of ideas as well as character/plot/situation.
- With extract questions particularly, don't meander loosely through the text – look at the outcomes from the extract, get them at or near the top of the essay and pull the arguments together with good selection and highlighting.
- Manipulate language in your essay, modifying as you proceed rather than crossing out words and phrases. Crossings out will betray indecision, while skilful manoeuvring will reflect well on you.
- The key unit of meaning is the sentence; your sentences need to be controlled and purposeful.
- Paragraphs are also important – they usually reflect the level of organization in an essay. Too few or short paragraphs betray problems with the authority and control of an argument. Use a paragraph for a definite purpose, such as discussing a character at a particular moment.
- Your conclusion, remember, came at the start of the essay! If you possibly can, end your essay with something consciously saved from earlier.
- Do not overrun your time on any question!

1.5.1 Prose – Contemporary

FOCUS ON THE EXAM

LI | **Unit 2**

GCSE English Literature Unit 2a

If you choose to do Unit 2a in English Literature, you will be asked to study a contemporary prose text. In the exam, you will answer two questions on this text. The first question (part (i)) will ask you to carry out a close reading of an extract from the text. The second question must be chosen from a choice of two tasks (parts (ii) and (iii)). This question will relate to the whole text.

Contemporary Prose

What does 'contemporary prose' mean?

These texts are all novels that have been written in recent times. They are written by people of the late **20th or early 21st century**, although the novels may be concerned with an earlier period. They may stretch imagination to the past and the future in interesting ways. In some ways, they force us to take stock of where we are now.

> **List features of the book you are studying that help you to pinpoint the time that it is set in.**

The setting

Where does the story take place? Does the writer hint at the place or describe it in detail? Is it a familiar kind of setting or somewhere more imaginative? Is there a particular setting (or location) or are there several? What is the importance of the setting to the story as a whole? Is the setting just part of the background? Does the setting create a mood or atmosphere? What is the mood or atmosphere of the story?

Childhood

Writers represent the experience of childhood in different ways. They may write a fairly straightforward account of reflective memories or try to show the details and feelings of childhood through the eyes and voice of a child.

> **Read the following extract closely. How does the writer convey the experience of childhood? Use the text to support your points.**

Paddy Clarke Ha Ha Ha

First there were more new houses. There was no one in them yet because they'd all flooded before they were finished. Past the houses was the fields with the hills, the one that had been dug up and stopped and grown over, where we built our huts. And over the hills was Bayside.

Bayside wasn't finished yet but it wasn't the building sites we were after this time. It was the shape of the place. It was mad. The roads were crooked. The garages weren't in the proper place. They were in blocks away from the houses. Down a path, into a yard, a fort made of garages. The place made no sense. We went there to get lost.

   - It's a labyrinth.
   - Labyrinth!
   - Labyrinth labyrinth labyrinth!

We charged through on our bikes. Bikes became important, our horses. We galloped through the garage yards and made it to the other side. I tied a rope to the handlebars and hitched my bike to a pole whenever I got off it. We parked our bikes on verges so they could graze. The rope got caught between the spokes of the front wheel; I went over the handlebars, straight over. it was over before I knew. The bike was on top of me. I was alone. I was okay. I wasn't even cut. We charged into the garages -

   -Woo wooo wooo wooo woo wooo wooo! And the garages captured our noise and made it bigger and grown-up. We escaped out the other end, out onto the street and back for a second attack.

> **Select an extract from the novel you are studying that focuses on issues of childhood. It could be an extract involving a minor character in the story. Explain what the writer is observing and commenting upon in the extract.**

Dilemma

Writers can get inside the heads of their characters. Characters might weigh up a problem or **dilemma** that faces them, and the reader may witness this very private struggle, observing the arguments and counter-arguments as they arise. This process often makes the reader more **sympathetic** to the character.

> **Read this extract from *About a Boy* and then explain the situation that Marcus faces in your own words.**

About a Boy

Marcus could see that. He could imagine that if they had never met him, Nicky and Mark would have had as much contact with Lee Hartley and the rest of them as Koala bears have with piranha fish. But now, because of him, the koala bears had fallen into the sea and the piranhas were taking an interest in them. Nobody had hurt them, not yet, and Marcus knew all about the stuff with sticks and stones and names. But insults were hurled in just the same way as missiles, if you thought about it, and if other people happened to be standing in the line of fire they got hit too. That's what had happened with Nicky and Mark: he had made them visible, he had turned them into targets, and if he was any kind of friend at all he'd take himself well away from them. It's just that he had nowhere else to go.

> **Select an extract from the novel that you are studying that shows a character facing a crucial decision. Explain the situation that the character is in in your own words.**

Crisis

Characters reach points in their story where things come to a head. This creates new problems for a character, but provides a turning point or crisis that sets the novel moving forward again for the reader.

> **Look at the extract below. What are the main character's thoughts and feelings?**

Heroes

Now each day when I wake up I know that this might be the day when Larry LaSalle will show up and I start to close doors. Not real doors but doors to the future. I take out the address and telephone number of Dr Adams in Kansas City and burn it in the kitchen sink. Next is the list of veterans' hospitals that Enrico handed to me when I left England. 'I'll be in one of them,' he told me, 'until I find the proper method of disposal.' I knew what he meant by disposal because I had already planned my own method when my mission was complete.

I watch the flames eating up the list of hospitals. Good bye Enrico.

The smell of ashes fills the air, a damp incense burning for Larry LaSalle's home-coming.

His second home-coming.

Closing my eyes, I think of Nicole and how his first home-coming during the war changed our lives forever.

> **Select an extract from the novel you are studying where a key character looks backwards at a part of his or her own past. What are the character's thoughts and feelings?**

The action

What happens in the story? What are the key events?

Now think about how they link together as a plot. Are there twists and cliff-hangers? Is the plot fast-moving or is there a steady build-up of suspense?

What period of time is covered by the story – a few days or less? A year or more? Does the writer create a mystery by holding back information from the reader? Does the writer deliberately complicate the story or is it a fairly simple forward-moving sequence of events? Is the story easy or difficult to believe in?

Forming a personal response

What is your considered personal response after reading the story? Have you learned anything from the text? Has it changed (or perhaps confirmed) your opinions in any way? What is your attitude to the writer after reading the story?

The narrator

Who tells the story? Is it a **first-person narrator** (a character in the story) or a **third-person narrator** (an observer of the action from outside the story)? Is the narrator an important part of the story you are studying? Does the narrator have a distinct voice with any obvious features of language, such as dialect? Does the storyteller involve the reader closely in the story? Does the storyteller have a clear attitude to events and characters?

Mystery

A first-person narrator in a novel essentially tells the story directly from the point of view of one of the characters. The reader becomes involved with the character and sees and hears everything from that character's point of view. This means information in the story is limited to what this character knows or experiences. Mystery can therefore be created by a writer's decision to use a first-person narrator.

> **How does the writer try to create mystery in the extract below? Refer to details in the text.**

Never Let Me Go

My name is Kathy H. I'm thirty-one years old, and I've been a carer for over eleven years. That sounds long enough, I know, but actually they want me to go on for another eight months, until the end of the year. That'll make it almost exactly twelve years. Now, I know my being a carer so long isn't necessarily because they think I'm fantastic at what I do. There are some really good carers who've been told to stop after just two or three years. And I can think of one carer at least who went on for all of fourteen years despite being a complete waste of space. So I'm not trying to boast. But then I do know for a fact they've been pleased with my work, and by and large, I have too. My donors have always tended to do much better than expected. Their recovery times have been impressive, and hardly any of them have been classified as 'agitated', even before forth donation. Okay, maybe I am boasting now.

> **Select an extract from the novel you are studying that is clouded in mystery. How does the writer create and sustain the mystery?**

Presenting character through action

A character can be presented strongly through his or her external actions as reported by the narrator. The choices and decisions a character makes are particularly important in telling us more about their character.

> **What do you learn about the character of Maggie from the extract from *Resistance* below?**

Resistance

She did not sit down. Albrecht and she spoke standing on the flagstones in the front room instead, like two battlefield generals meeting at dawn to negotiate the day's engagement. The room smelt of solidified fat and old fire, cold ashes shifting under the grate in the breeze from the opened door.

Maggie made herself clear. They would not give the Germans anything. Food, supplies of any kind. The government had forbidden it and she wanted Captain Wolfram to know this now, to avoid any confusion. She would make sure that everyone in the valley stayed away from The Court while the soldiers were here. In return she wanted the Captain's assurance again that he and his men would leave them undisturbed and allow them to get on with their work of running the farms.

> **Find an extract from the novel you are studying that reveals the character of someone by the way the character behaves.**

The characters

Some questions to consider:

- Who are the main characters in the story?
- Are there interesting minor characters who appear in the story?
- Is there one character who stands out above the rest as the focus of the reader's interest?
- How does the writer present the character(s) to us – through description, tone, dialogue or actions?
- What do you find interesting about the main character(s)?
- Are there any striking relationships or conflicts between characters?
- How do the characters develop and change through the story?

1.5.2 Prose – Literary Heritage

GCSE English Literature Unit 2b

If you choose to do Unit 2b in English Literature, you will be asked to study a heritage prose text. In the exam, you will answer two questions. The first question (part (i)) will require a close reading of an extract. The second question will need to be selected from a choice of two (parts (ii) and (iii)) and will relate to the whole text.

What is Literary Heritage Prose?

Literary Heritage Prose includes some of the great British novels of the past. Many of these novels have strong moral themes that are still relevant to life in the present. They include stories that are simply part of the nation's consciousness, characters that are as well-known as famous people, and settings that give us clear images of social history. Literary Heritage Prose also goes beyond fiction - into the realms of autobiography and other significant non-fiction prose works.

Recalling the past

The act of remembering can result in very clear descriptions and stories, but can also involve looking through a haze to a distant point in the past. The writer may engage in a very definite effort to remember, or use flashbacks to establish a sharp impression of past events. The reader may not think to question the precision of the writer's detailed memories.

Look at the following extract. How does the writer retell the memory from Summer 1934?

Ash on a Young Man's Sleeve

Uncle Bertie, I remember, in the old days…back in 1934…in the summer of the Heat-Wave 1934…I remember…

It was very hot and they sat under the apple tree playing cards: mother, Aunt Cecile, Leo and Leo's friend Jimmy Ford. Uncle Isidore lay asleep in the deck-chair, dirty and dishevelled as usual, and I rested on the lawn, reading. Mother liked to have Uncle Isidore in the summer garden for all the insects in the vicinity were attracted to him, ignoring the other customers who only smelt of mere soap and pedestrian water. I looked up watching the excited insects fly about Uncle Isidore who lay back asleep, unperturbed, as he exuded mysterious smells – odours that proliferated exotically in Isidore's ragged clothes, ragged hair, ragtime beard.

The card-players talked about the theatre. Uncle Bertie strode through the drawing-room, into the garden, a huge figure of a man, with strong black hair, blazing grey eyes.

'Actresses,' Aunt Cecile was saying, 'are women who call everybody "darling" to obviate silly errors. Ah look,' she added, seeing Bertie, 'here's Bertie, isn't he splendid?' But Uncle bertie was angry: he spoke in his special booming voice. 'Nobody, nobody insults our family and gets away with it.'

'What's the matter, what's the matter?' asked Uncle Isidore waking up startled.

Select an extract from the text you are studying that deals with the act of remembering. How does the writer present this?

The writer's skills

What do you appreciate and admire about the way the writer has written the story? Which writing skills or techniques stand out as memorable? The writer may appear to display special skills when describing people and places or when presenting dialogue, feelings and attitudes. The writer may be particularly skilled at organizing a plot cleverly. Do the writers use wit? How does he or she create tension and atmosphere? Does the writer have a style of writing that has particular features? Is it noted for its rich range of language, description, and imagery? Is it particularly clear and direct?

Setting

Setting gives a sense of place to a story, and without it the story would be unbalanced. The setting leads the writer and then the reader into the world of the novel. The setting contributes to the mood and atmosphere of the story. It includes the localized environment, the time of day, the time of year and very often the climate.

Setting is important in the extract from *A Christmas Carol* below.

A Christmas Carol

Once upon a time - of all the good days in the year, on Christmas Eve - old Scrooge sat busy in his counting-house. It was cold, bleak, biting weather: foggy withal: and he could hear the people in the court outside, go wheezing up and down, beating their hands upon their breasts, and stamping their feet upon the pavement stones to warm them. The city clocks had only just gone three, but it was quite dark already - it had not been light all day - and candles were flaring in the windows of the neighbouring offices, like ruddy smears upon the palpable brown air. The fog came pouring in at every chink and keyhole, and was so dense without, that although the court was of the narrowest, the houses opposite were mere phantoms. To see the dingy cloud come drooping down, obscuring everything, one might have thought that Nature lived hard by, and was brewing on a large scale.

Select an extract from the text you are studying that describes an important setting. Write about its importance in detail, using your own words as far as possible.

The time in which the text was written/set

Consider your text. Is the story set in modern times or in the past? How distant from today does the story feel? If it is a pre-1914 story, what does it reveal about the time in which it was written? Are there any features of traditional storytelling – perhaps a more leisurely style? If it is a post-1914 story, does it reflect a more modern world? Does the text include any features of modern storytelling; perhaps a more direct, urgent style?

Incident and impact

Moments of great drama occur in the best novels. Such events can provoke an element of shock and horror, especially when events occur out of the blue. Characters may behave in a way that betrays bad taste or bad judgement, leaving the reader disappointed with them. When this occurs the reader may feel sudden detachment from the character or may have less sympathy for them.

> **How does the writer create a sense of horror in the lines below?**

Lord of the Flies

Jack, his face smeared with clay reached the top first and hailed Ralph excitedly, with lifted spear.

'Look! We've killed a pig - we stole up on them - we got in a circle –'

Voices broke from the hunters.

'We got in a circle –'

'We crept up –'

'The pig squealed –'

The twins stood with the pig swinging between them, dropping black gouts on the rock. They seemed to share one wide, ecstatic grin. Jack had too many things to tell Ralph at once. Instead, he danced a step or two, then remembered his dignity and stood still, grinning. He noticed blood on his hands and grimaced distastefully, looked for something on which to clean them, then wiped them on his shorts and laughed.

Ralph spoke.

'You let the fire out.'

Jack checked, vaguely irritated by this irrelevance but too happy to let it worry him.

> **Select an extract from the novel that you are studying that deals with a shocking incident. How does the writer convey the drama of the incident?**

Key scenes and events

What are the key scenes or events in your novel? Why is each one important?

Now think about how the main characters behave before and after these key scenes and events. Do your opinions of any of the characters change as a result?

A touch of style

Style takes many forms, but, whatever style a novelist adopts, he or she is trying to use the best possible words for the occasion. The novelist is in absolute control of a wide variety of sentence types, all used for precise effect, rather than for show. Styles of writing from the literary heritage prose texts are likely, though not certain, to be classical, traditional and elaborate, perhaps even provoking the word 'stylish'.

> **Read the following extract from *Pride and Prejudice*. How does the writer's style help to convey the occasion of the ball?**

Pride and Prejudice

Mr Bingley had soon made himself acquainted with all the principal people in the room; he was lively and unreserved, danced every dance, was angry that the ball closed so early, and talked of giving one himself at Netherfield. Such amiable qualities must speak for themselves. What a contrast between him and his friend! Mr Darcy danced only once with Mrs Hurst, and once with Miss Bingley, declined being introduced to any other lady, and spent the rest of the evening in walking about the room, speaking occasionally to one of his own party. His character was decided. He was the proudest, most disagreeable man in the world, and every body hoped that he would never come there again. Amongst the most violent against him was Mrs Bennet, whose dislike of his general behaviour, was sharpened into particular resentment, by his having slighted one of her daughters.

> **Select an extract from the novel that you are studying that has a contrasting style to the one in the lines above. Compare and contrast both pieces of writing.**

The ending

Endings are just as important as openings. How does the novel you are studying end? Is it a satisfying ending that suits the type of story? Does the story end as you expected? Is it an open ending? Does the writer leave questions unanswered about characters and themes? Does the writer pull all the loose ends together at the end to complete the story? Has the mood and atmosphere changed during the story?

Confused emotions

The great British novelists have created memorable, emotionally rounded and convincing characters. The third-person narrator is able to share with the reader the full picture of good fortune or misfortune as it affects key characters. The feelings are expressed explicitly, generally within the context of traditional Christian values.

> **How does the writer show Silas's state of mind in the following lines?**

Silas Marner

Silas said 'Good-bye, and thank you, kindly,' as he opened the door for Dolly, but he couldn't help feeling relieved when she was gone—relieved that he might weave again and moan at his ease. Her simple view of life and its comforts, by which she had tried to cheer him, was only like a report of unknown objects, which his imagination could not fashion. The fountains of human love and divine faith had not yet been unlocked, and his soul was still the shrunken rivulet, with only this difference, that its little groove of sand was blocked up, and it wandered confusedly against dark obstruction.

And so, notwithstanding the honest persuasions of Mr Macey and Dolly Winthrop, Silas spent his Christmas-day in loneliness, eating his meat in sadness of heart, though the meat had come to him as a neighbourly present.

> **Select an extract from the text that you are studying that shows a character in a state of confusion. How does the writer show the character's range of feelings?**

The writer's ideas

What themes is the writer interested in? What is the writer perhaps trying to say about life, people, the world at large? If the writer lived in the past, are the ideas still relevant? In what ways have attitudes changed (or are changing)? What is the writer trying to help you to understand? Is the writer optimistic (full of hope) or pessimistic (not hopeful) about the ideas he or she is expressing in the story?

1.5.3 Drama – Literary Heritage

GCSE English Literature Unit 2a

If you choose to do Unit 2a in English Literature, you will be asked to study a heritage drama text. In the exam, you will answer two questions on this text. The first question (part (i)) will require a close reading of an extract. The second question must be chosen from two options (parts (ii) and (iii)). This question will relate to the whole text.

What is Literary Heritage Drama?

There have been just a few great ages of British drama. The first was the Elizabethan age, in which William Shakespeare and many other playwrights came to fame. Not all of the plays written then are still popular in the theatre today, but many that still are were written by Shakespeare. The late 19th to early 20th century again produced outstanding plays for the public at large, while the 1950s saw a breakthrough of plays about the lives of ordinary people.

Downfall

The high drama towards the end of a Shakespeare tragedy leaves an audience pulling in vain against the doom of the situation. The tragic hero has the power to avoid the tragic end, but inevitably is drawn towards his fate.

Look at the following scene from *Othello*. How does Shakespeare make this dramatic moment in the play between Othello and Desdemona so ominous?

Othello

DESDEMONA : Who's there? Othello?

OTHELLO: Ay, Desdemona.

DESDEMONA : Will you come to bed, my lord?

OTHELLO : Have you pray'd tonight, Desdemona?

DESDEMONA: Ay, my lord.

OTHELLO : If you bethink yourself of any crime
Unreconcil'd as yet to heaven and grace,
Solicit for it straight.

DESDEMONA: Alack, my lord, what may you mean by that?

ORTHELLO : Well, do it, and be brief: I will walk by:
I would not kill thy unprepared spirit;
No—heaven forfend!—I would not kill thy soul.

DESDEMONA : Talk you of killing?

OTHELLO : Ay, I do.

DESDEMONA : Then heaven
have mercy on me!

OTHELLO : Amen, with all my heart!

Select a short exchange of high drama between characters in the play that you are studying. How does the writer create the high drama at this point?

The action

What happens in the play? What are the key events? How do they link together to form the plot? Are there twists and cliff-hangers? Is the plot fast-moving or is there a steady build-up of suspense? What period of time is covered by the action – a few days or less? A year or more? Does the writer create a mystery by holding back information from the audience? Does the writer deliberately complicate the action or is it a fairly simple forward-moving sequence of events? Is the action easy or difficult to believe in?

Revelation

Extra plot details or layers of a character can be revealed at any point of a play. The comfortable defiance of a confident personality can be shattered when a new piece of information is fed into the action.

An Inspector Calls

BIRLING : Is there any good reason why my wife should answer questions from you, Inspector?

INSPECTOR : Yes, a very good reason. You'll remember that Mr Croft told us – quite truthfully, I believe – that he hadn't spoken to or seen Eva Smith since last September. But Mrs Birling spoke to and saw her only two weeks ago.

SHEILA : *(astonished)* Mother!

BIRLING :   Is this true?

MRS B :   *(after a pause)* Yes, quite true.

INSPECTOR : She appealed to your organization for help?

MRS B :   Yes.

INSPECTOR : Not as Eva Smith?

MRS B :   No. Nor as Daisy Renton.

INSPECTOR : As what then?

MRS B :   First, she called herself Mrs Birling—

BIRLING :   *(astounded)* Mrs Birling!

MRS B :   Yes, I think it was simply a piece of gross impertinence – quite deliberate – and naturally that was one of the things that prejudiced me against her case.

BIRLING :   And I should think so! Damn impudence!

INSPECTOR : You admit to being prejudiced against her case?

MRS B :   Yes.

SHEILA :   Mother, she's just died a horrible death – don't forget.

MRS B :   I'm very sorry. But I think she had only herself to blame.

INSPECTOR : Was it owing to your influence as the most prominent member of the committee, that help was refused the girl?

MRS B :   Possibly.

INSPECTOR : Was it or was it not your influence?

MRS B :   *(stung)* Yes it was. I didn't like her manner. She'd impertinently made use of our name, though she pretended afterwards it just happened to be the first she thought of. She had to admit, after I began questioning her, that she had no claim to the name, that she wasn't married, and that the story she told at first – about a husband who'd deserted her – was quite false. It didn't take me long to get the truth – or some of the truth – out of her.

How is the true character of Mrs Birling revealed in this scene?

> **Select an extract from a play that you are studying that reveals the truth about a character. How does the writer present the character?**

The characters

Who are the main characters in the play? Do any interesting minor characters appear in the play? Is there one character who stands out above the rest as the main focus of our interest? How does the writer present the character(s) to us? Does the writer use description, personality, dialogue, actions or a combination of techniques? What do you find interesting about the main character(s)? Are there any interesting relationships or conflicts between characters? How do the characters develop and change throughout the play?

Hostility

Nothing represents the excitement of drama better than a head-to-head confrontation between characters. When the underdog faces up to the bully, the triumph is enjoyed by all.

> **How does the writer present the confrontation between Maggie and Hobson in the lines below?**

Hobson's Choice

MAGGIE : I'm thirty and I'm marrying Willie Mossop. And now I'll tell you my terms.

HOBSON : You're in a nice position to state terms, my lass.

MAGGIE : You will pay my man, Will Mossop, the same wages as before. And as for me, I've given you the better part of twenty years of work without wages. I'll work eight hours a day in the future and you will pay me fifteen shillings by the week.

HOBSON : Do you think I'm made of brass?

MAGGIE : You'll soon be made of mess that you are if you let Willie go. And if Willie goes, I go. That's what you've got to face.

HOBSON : I might face it , Maggie. Shop hands are cheap.

MAGGIE : Cheap ones are cheap. The sort you'd have to watch all day, and you'd feel happy helping them to tie up parcels and sell laces with Tudsbury and Heeler and Minns supping their ale without you. I'm value to you, so's my man; and you can boast it at the 'Moonraker's' that your daughter Maggie's made the strangest, finest match a woman's made this fifty year. And you can put your hand in your pocket and do what I propose.

HOBSON : I'll show you what I propose, Maggie. *(He lifts the trap and calls)*
Will Mossop! *(He places his hat on the counter and unbuckles his belt)*
I cannot leather you, my lass. You're female, and exempt, but I can
leather him. Come up, Will Mossop.
(Willie comes up the trap and closes it)
You've taken with my Maggie, I hear. *(He conceals the strap)*

WILLIE : Nay, I've not. She's done the taking up.

HOBSON : Well, Willie, either way, you've fallen on misfortune. Love's led you
astray, and I feel bound to put you right. *(He shows the strap)*

**Select an extract from the play you are studying in which a
confrontation comes to a head. How does the writer present the
confrontation?**

The setting

Where does the action take place? Does the writer describe it in detail? Is the stage
expected to be very precisely arranged? What is the importance of the setting to the
story as a whole? Is the setting just part of the background? Does the setting create a
mood or atmosphere? What is the mood or atmosphere of the play? What theatrical
tricks or surprises are evident?

Disagreement

Characters can represent ordinary lives. People who know each other engage in petty squabbling. The disagreement however can have greater significance. The lack of self-awareness and wisdom shown by the characters could or perhaps should make the audience more self-aware and wise.

How does the writer present the disagreement between Helen and Jo?

A Taste of Honey

HELEN : What's the matter with you? What are you trying to hide?

JO : Nothing.

HELEN : Don't try to kid me. What is it? Come on, let's see.

JO : It's nothing. Let go of me. You're hurting.

HELEN : What's this?

JO : A ring.

HELEN : I can see it's a ring. Who gave it to you?

JO : A friend of mine.

HELEN : Who? Come on. Tell me.

JO : You're hurting me.

(Helen breaks the cord and gets the ring)

HELEN : You should have sewn some buttons on your pyjamas if you didn't want me to see. Who gave it to you?

JO : My boyfriend. He asked me to marry him.

HELEN : Well, you silly little bitch. You mean that lad you've been knocking about with while we've been away?

JO : Yes

HELEN : I could choke you.

JO : You've already had a damn good try.

HELEN : You haven't known him five minutes. Has he really asked you to marry him?

Jo : Yes.

HELEN : Well, thank God for divorce courts! I suppose just because I'm getting married you think you should.

Select an extract from the play you are studying that shows a disagreement between two characters. How does the writer present the disagreement?

The ending

How does the play end? Is it a satisfying ending that suits the type of play? Does the play end as you expected? Does it have an open ending? Does the writer leave questions unanswered about characters and themes? Does the writer pull all the loose ends together at the end to complete the play? Has the mood and atmosphere changed during the play?

Soliloquies

A soliloquy is a speech spoken by a character alone on stage. Writers often use soliloquies to reveal a character's honest views.

> **Explain in your own words what Beatrice is saying in the lines below.**

Much Ado About Nothing

BEATRICE

(Coming forward) What fire is in mine ears? Can this be true?
Stand I condemn'd for pride and scorn so much?
Contempt, farewell; and maiden pride, adieu.
No glory lives behind the back of such.
And, Benedick, love on. I will requite thee,
Taming my wild heart to thy loving hand.
If thou dost love, my kindness shall incite thee
To bind our loves up in a holy band.
For others say thou dost deserve, and I
Believe it better than reportingly.

> **Select a speech from the play that you are studying that expresses a character's honest thoughts about a relationship. Explain how the character expresses those thoughts.**

The time in which the play was written/is set

Is the play set in modern times or in the past? How distant from today does the play appear? If it is a Shakespeare play, what does it reveal about the attitudes of his age? In what ways are Shakespeare's characters timeless; showing unchanging human characteristics? If it is a post-1914 play, does it represent a modern world? Is there a particularly modern conflict or dilemma at the heart of the play? Do the characters behave in a way that people of bygone ages would fail to understand?

1.5.4 Drama – Contemporary

GCSE English Literature Unit 2b

If you choose to do Unit 2b in English Literature, you will be asked to study a contemporary drama text. In the exam, you will answer two questions on this text. The first question (part (i)) will require a close reading of an extract from the text. The second question must be chosen from two options (parts (ii) and (iii)). This question will relate to the whole text.

What is 'contemporary' drama?

Contemporary drama deals with modern issues and it tends to be controversial. It often faces-up to disturbing topics. In reality, it overlaps with literary heritage drama, simply because categories such as these are never absolute; it is all a matter of opinion! The plays sometimes deal with the here and now as the writer witnesses it, but may also look back a decade or so, or a generation, to allow for reflection and perspective.

The structure of the play

How many acts and scenes are there in the play? Is there a prologue and/or epilogue? Is the play heavy or light on stage directions? Is there a narrator (or a character with the role of narrator)? Do any characters speak their thoughts at length in a soliloquies? Is there a clear conflict of ideas running through the play? Is there more than one plot (a main plot with sub-plots)? Are there key moments of dramatic irony, when the audience understands what is going on, but not the character(s)? How does the play build-up to its climax? How is the conflict resolved?

Lives

Drama can throw up interesting historical perspectives. A modern drama can make sharp contrasts with the past and can focus on the issues of passing time. The lives of ordinary people are often properly valued, even if open to criticism, in a documentary-style approach.

> **Look at the scene below. How does the dramatist reveal the themes of the play in this extract?**

My Mother Said I Never Should

The backyard of Doris's terrace house in Oldham, early April 1987. Doris is eighty-seven and wears a floral overall. Margaret is fifty-six and dressed in a sensible suit she wears to work, wearing an apron she has borrowed from Doris. They are chatting as they come out of the back kitchen door. Margaret carrying a tray of small geraniums in pots, Doris carrying a tray and kneeler. They kneel beside a tub and a bag of potting compost.

DORIS :   See dear, all those are from one plant I bought with me from
                 Cheadle Hulme.

MARGARET :   I've had mine in the kitchen all winter, but they've not done so
                 well.

DORIS :   Oh you seem to have cut them right down until they're just dry
                 sticks, then all of a sudden, it seems, they start producing new
                 leaves.

MARGARET :   They'll look lovely in this tub.

DORIS :   I've had a postcard from Rosie. She and Jackie seem to be having
                 a lovely time.

MARGARET :   Yes. It's very quiet at home.

Pause

(Margaret continues planting a geranium in the tub.)

DORIS :   You look thinner. Are you eating properly?

MARGARET :   What do you mean?

DORIS :   Don't crowd the roots – well – you coming all the way from
                 London like this – on a Tuesday!

MARGARET :   Can't I even come and see you for the day without –

DORIS :   Usually you're so busy, at that office… never have time to come
                 and visit.

MARGARET :   Yes, well I took the day off!

DORIS :   No need to snap, dear.

Pause

(Margaret digs a hole.)

**Select an extract from the play that you are studying which embraces
some of the themes of the whole play. How does the dramatist deal
with these themes within the extract?**

Attitudes

Contrasting attitudes across generations are frequently impossible to resolve. They often represent the idealism of youth versus the cynicism of older people. They can also represent the blindness of one party and the stubbornness of the other. These differences might also mask deep-rooted feelings.

> **Select an extract from the play that you are studying that shows a conflict between people of different generations. How does the writer present the conflict?**

The opening scene(s)

How does the play start? What is in the very first scene? Is it a low-key or a highly dramatic opening? How are you drawn into the action? What holds your attention? How much does the writer tell you? Is it possible to tell how the plot will develop?

Control

Control, power and influence are at the centre of drama. This applies to plays about kings and queens, and also to plays about ordinary people. Conflict, opposition and struggle are closely related too, and are also evident in plays that operate on a domestic, humble level.

> **How does the writer present Mary's situation in the following lines?**

Be My Baby

(Study. Mrs Adams sits opposite Matron. Mary stands by her side.)

MATRON : So her condition came to light…
MRS ADAMS : Yesterday, Matron.
MATRON : And she was last unwell….
MRS ADAMS : September.
MATRON : Seven months?
MRS ADAMS : She let out her clothes and took Mother for a fool.
MATRON : Has your doctor verified?
MRS ADAMS : There wasn't time.
MATRON : May I take his details…

MRS ADAMS :	Why?
MATRON :	To send for her notes.
MRS ADAMS :	But he bowls with her father.
MATRON :	Who hasn't been told.
MRS ADAMS :	And won't be, with respect. He's put her on a pedestal, you see.
MATRON :	You know why you're here, Mary?
MARY :	Yes, Matron.
MATRON :	Then you know what you've done?
MRS ADAMS :	She knows far too much in my book.

(Matron takes notes as Mary replies.)

MATRON :	Full name?
MARY :	Mary Elizabeth Adams.
MATRON :	Date of birth?
MARY :	I'm not sure, exactly. I haven't seen the doctor.
MATRON :	Your birthday.
MRS ADAMS :	Pay attention, Mary.
MARY :	I'm sorry. March the first, 1945.

Select an extract from the play that you are studying that shows characters trying to control other characters. How does the writer convey this?

The writer's ideas

What themes is the writer interested in? What is the writer perhaps trying to say about life, people and the world at large? If the play was written in the past, are the ideas still relevant? In what ways have attitudes changed (or are changing)? What is the writer trying to get you to understand? Is the writer optimistic (full of hope) or pessimistic (not hopeful) about the ideas he or she is expressing in the play?

The writer's skills

What do you appreciate and admire about the way the writer has created the play? Which dramatic skills or techniques stand out as memorable? Does the writer appear to have special skills in visual drama, characterization, scenes of conflict or the presentation of feelings and attitudes (getting under the skin of characters)? Is the writer skilful when it comes to creating memorable minor characters, organizing a plot cleverly or using theatrical effects? Does the writer have wit? Does the writer create suspense?

Discussion

Characters can become engaged in intelligent discussion on stage. This may mark them out as clever and confident at the time, but uncertainty and discomfort is never far away. A play will cut through to the simple challenge of the truth and the moral position of individuals.

Look at the extract below. How does the writer make the discussion interesting and dramatic?

The History Boys

HECTOR :   I didn't teach you and Wittgenstein didn't screw it out of his very guts in order for you to turn it into a dinky formula. I thought that you of all people were bright enough to see that.

DAKIN :   I do see it, sir. Only I don't agree with it. Not… not any more.

TIMMS :   Sir.

HECTOR :   *(head in hands)* Yes?

TIMMS :   You told us once… it was to do with the trenches, sir… that one person's death tells you more than a thousand. When people are dying like flies, you said, that is what they are dying like.

POSNER :   Except that these weren't just dying. They were being processed. What is different is the process.

IRWIN :   Good.

HECTOR :   No, not good.
               Posner is not making a *point*.
               He is speaking from the heart.

DAKIN :   So? Supposing we get a question on Hitler and the Second War and we take your line, sir, that this is not a crazed lunatic but a statesman.

HECTOR :   A statesman?

IRWIN :   Not a statesman, Dakin, a politician. I wouldn't say statesman.

DAKIN :   Politician, then, and one erratically perhaps, but still discernibly operating within the framework of traditional German foreign policy….

IRWIN :   Yes?

DAKIN :   … and we go on to say, in accordance with this line, that the
               death camps have to be seen in the context of this policy.

Pause

IRWIN :   I think that would be… inexpedient.

HECTOR :   Inexpedient? Inexpedient?

IRWIN :   I don't think it's true, for a start…

SCRIPPS :   But what has truth got to do with it? I thought that we'd already
               decided that for the purposes of this examination truth is, if not
               an irrelevance, then so relative as just to amount to another
               point of view.

HECTOR :   Why can you not simply condemn the camps outright as an
               unprecedented horror?

               (*There is slight embarrassment.*)

Select an extract from the play you are studying that shows a character being challenged in discussion. How does the writer make the scene interesting and dramatic?

Decisions

In drama, the course of people's lives can be affected by one momentous decision. A drama can be created out of this decision: the characters' fate is set. Often, the decision that seems to be a solution to a problem can set a chain of events in motion.

> **How does the writer convey the dramatic decision in the lines below?**

Blood Brothers

MRS LYONS : Hello, Mrs J. How are you?

(There is no reply)

(Registering the silence) Mrs J? Anything wrong?

MRS JOHNSTONE : I had it all worked out.

MRS LYONS : What's the matter?

MRS JOHNSTONE : We were just getting straight.

MRS LYONS : Why don't you sit down.

MRS JOHNSTONE : With one more baby we could have managed. But not with two. The welfare have already been on to me. They say I'm incapable of controllin' the kids I've already got. They say I should put them into care. But I won't. I love the bones of every one of them. I'll even love these two when they come along. But like they say at the Welfare, kids can't live on love alone.

MRS LYONS : Twins? You're expecting twins?

The NARRATOR enters.

NARRATOR : How quickly an idea, planted, can take root and grow into a plan. The thought conceived in this very room grew as surely as a seed, in a mother's womb.

The NARRATOR exits.

MRS LYONS : *(almost inaudibly)* Give one to me.

MRS JOHNSTONE : What?

> **Select an extract from the play that you have been studying that shows a moment when characters make a critical decision. How does the writer convey the importance of those lines?**

The reader/audience

What is your considered personal response after watching and studying the play? Have you learned anything from the play? Has it changed (or perhaps confirmed) your opinions in any way? How did you feel watching it and, now, having studied it? What is your attitude to the writer after studying the play?

How is poetry and drama assessed at GCSE?

Does the response to the text...

- ❑ show some personal response and general knowledge of the story?
- ❑ show some understanding of main features and selection of relevant detail?
- ❑ discuss characters and relationships thoughtfully, probe the sub-text, and select and evaluate relevant textual details?
- ❑ make assured selection and use of relevant detail, with thoughtful judgements on characters and relationships?
- ❑ consistently handle it with confidence, with an overview and ability to move from the specific to the general?

Are there...

- ❑ generalized comments about language, structure and form?
- ❑ simple comments on particular features of style and structure?
- ❑ comments about how different aspects of style and structure create effects, meanings and ideas?
- ❑ assured comments exploring meaning and appreciating language and structure?
- ❑ assured and developed analytical comments on stylistic features?

Are there...

- ❑ simple points of comparison when required, and simple preferences?
- ❑ straightforward links and connections between texts, and references to obvious features of similarity and difference?
- ❑ comparisons and some evaluation of subject, theme, character and the impact of texts?
- ❑ sustained explanations of the relevance and impact of detailed connections and comparisons between texts?
- ❑ subtle points of comparison and points that show confident exploration of links?

Is there...

- ❑ a range of simple comments on the background of the text?
- ❑ a limited awareness of social/cultural and historical contexts?
- ❑ a clear grasp of social/cultural and historical contexts?
- ❑ a variety of clear comments on the importance of social/cultural and historical contexts showing awareness of literary tradition?
- ❑ a clear selection of details from the text that have been related to the literary background and a clear understanding of social/cultural and historical contexts?

Is the expression (the grammar, punctuation and spelling)...

- ❑ likely to impede communication on occasions?
- ❑ reasonably clear with a basic structure, with errors not too intrusive but specialist vocabulary limited?
- ❑ mainly clear and fluent and quite well-structured, with occasional errors in spelling or punctuation and specialist vocabulary used appropriately?
- ❑ clear and fluent and the answer well-structured with few errors in grammar, punctuation and spelling and appropriate use of specialist vocabulary?

Preparing for the exam

Here are the relevant details for this part of the assessment, including the relevant Assessment Objectives for the English Literature specification.

 GCSE ENGLISH LITERATURE UNIT 2a: Literary heritage drama and contemporary prose

GCSE ENGLISH LITERATURE UNIT 2b: Contemporary drama and literary heritage prose

Individual texts in context (40%)

Examination

You will answer **two** questions on **each** of your chosen texts. The first question (part (i)) will require a close reading of an extract. The second question will offer a choice of two tasks (part (ii)) and (part (iii)). Both options will relate to the text as a whole.

AOI

●   Respond to texts critically and imaginatively; select and evaluate relevant textual detail to illustrate and support interpretations.

AO2

●   Explain how language, structure and form contribute to writers' presentation of ideas, themes and settings.

AO4

●   Relate texts to their social, cultural and historical contexts; explain how texts have been influential and significant to self and other readers in different contexts and at different times.

What is an essay?

An **essay** is a continuous piece of writing on a subject. In English Literature, you would not expect to see subheadings, separate sections or illustrations in an essay; therefore using **paragraphs** is an essential part of building the structure of your response.

Discursive writing in English Literature requires you to organize your own selection of facts and opinions to respond to a fairly open task or question. In fact, a discursive essay is a **one-way discussion**, so you have to work hard to keep to the question.

In a **closed-book exam**, you should show your knowledge and understanding of your set novel and set play by **direct quotation** or **other types of evidence**.

Direct reference and detailed knowledge can be shown through confident use of names, reference to specific details, paraphrase and very short, embedded quotations (usually a word or a phrase).

Reading a text independently

You will be a much stronger English Literature exam candidate if you are able and willing to read and study your books at home. If you do get to read the set texts independently before your teacher introduces them in class, keep a record of your response to each text and be confident that these will be relevant and useful to you later. The following questions attempt to help you become an active reader and a proper student. Reading a text independently is the opposite of spoon-feeding!

The Plot

- What happens at the start of the text? What do you think of the opening?
- How do you expect the plot to develop? What are the key stages of the plot?
- How do you expect the story to end? What do you think of the ending?
- Are any questions left unanswered?

The Characters

- How important is each character in the plot?
- How do some of the characters change as the story develops?
- Are there any moments when you feel strongly for or against particular characters?
- Do the various locations/settings of the story cause the characters to behave differently?

Themes

- What are the main themes and how do they develop?
- How do the main characters demonstrate these themes in their behaviour?
- What is the writer trying to say about these themes?

The Writer

- Do you notice anything that stands out about the writer's style of writing?
- Is there anything interesting about the way the writer has arranged and organized the story?

Writing an exam essay on prose or drama

- Divide your time wisely between each question on the paper. Read each of the questions through quickly at the start of the exam. Let your subconscious mind do some work.
- Answer the question, which means do the task as set.
- Start at the sharp end; your first impressions are vital. Think before you start.
- Give the examiner something positive to tick in the first sentence.
- Make the examiner think, "high grade?" after the first paragraph.
- Get the writer in your essay early – see the writer as part of the discussion.
- Quotations should be short, frequent and integrated. The standard length of a quote should be the 'phrase' i.e. less than a full sentence. However, the 'single word' quote may be appropriate and so might a whole sentence occasionally.

- Echo (or refer back to) the question in every paragraph. Often, one word will do it. If none of your paragraph ties with the question, then you have drifted away. If so, don't panic, but return to the trail promptly.
- Get to the heart of the text or character at the start of the question. Have enthusiasm and respect for each text.
- Conveying a developed overview of each text should be a priority, however localized the extract you are working with. Don't leave the exam regretting missed opportunities to discuss key meanings of the texts – it's your chance. Make your essay work on the level of ideas as well as character/plot/situation.
- With extract questions particularly, don't meander loosely through the text – look at the outcomes from the extract, get them at or near the top of the essay and pull the arguments together with good selection and highlighting.
- Manipulate language in your essay modifying as you proceed rather than crossing out words and phrases. Crossings out will betray indecision, while skilful manoeuvring will reflect well on you.
- The key unit of meaning is the sentence; your sentences need to be controlled and purposeful.
- Paragraphs are also important – they usually reflect the level of organization in an essay. Too few or short paragraphs betray problems with the authority and control of an argument. Use a paragraph for a definite purpose, such as discussing a character at a particular moment.
- Your conclusion, remember, came at the start of the essay! If you possibly can, end your essay with something consciously saved from earlier.
- Do not overrun your time on any question!

The importance of English writing skills

The quality of your writing skills plays a significant part in your performance. Good control of your expression will get the examiner on your side and will contribute to the overall judgement of your work.

It will be an advantage if you:
- communicate clearly
- organize your ideas using sentences and paragraphs
- use a range of sentence structures effectively
- use a wide range of vocabulary
- use the grammar of standard English
- use accurate spelling
- use accurate punctuation
- present work clearly and neatly.

Most important of all, your writing should have a sense of purpose – in other words, answer the question as set. Do not repeat the essay you wrote in the mock exam on last year's paper, and do not offload thoughtlessly, everything you know about your set books. Ensure everything you write is relevant to the question!

DRAMA TERMS

Stage directions are instructions from the playwright for the actor and reader which are usually printed in italics and often also in brackets.

Dramatic effects includes anything which happens during a play to produce a response in members of the audience.

Exits and entrances are significant in a play, because scenes change when someone leaves and someone else arrives. You see the characters in different situations.

Dialogue is the conversation of a play (the words spoken by characters to each other) overheard by the audience.

Action is, in one sense, anything that happens in a play. However, it may be useful to see it as anything beyond the words spoken in a play – the movement, the physical action.

Conflict is needed in any worthwhile drama (even comedy). It is the disagreement, the tension, the opposition, the argument, the fighting between characters that drives the play on.

An **aside** is a comment made by a character that is intended to be heard by the audience, but not by the other characters on stage.

The **climax** of a play (or part of a play) is the peak of the play in terms of dramatic action or emotion.

Dramatic irony is a situation when the audience knows more about the events and exchanges on stage than the characters do.

A **soliloquy** is a speech spoken by a character who is alone on stage.

A **director** supervises and instructs actors who are appearing in the production of a play

Empathy is the ability to understand and share the feelings of others

Sympathy is the feeling of pity and sorrow for someone else's misfortune

A **soliloquy** is the speaking of thoughts out loud by a character in a play

A **monologue** is a long speech by one actor (character) in a play

Chapter 2.1   Creative Writing

FOCUS ON CONTROLLED ASSESSMENT   LA UNIT 3   E UNIT 3

GCSE English Language Unit 3

The writing requirements will include a piece of **descriptive writing** and a **narrative/expressive task** based on the tasks supplied by WJEC.

For example:

Descriptive:	*Describe the scene on a beach or at a funfair.*
Narrative/expressive:	*Write a story with the following title: Revenge.*

GCSE English Unit 3

The writing requirements will include a piece of **first person** and a piece of **third person narrative** writing.

For example:

First person:	*Often in life things do not turn out as we expect them. Recount an experience that you have had where you were surprised about the outcome.*
Third person:	*Write a story in the third person about a situation where a person is put in danger or a difficult circumstance.*

Whenever you write, you have to dream up words and put them into sentences. All writing requires you to be creative. **Creative writing** perhaps requires a little more of your imagination than some other types of writing, but the best imaginative writing is based on the possibilities of real life and experience: people and places, situations and stories, descriptions and narratives. The tasks in this chapter will show you the distinctions between descriptive and narrative writing. They will also demonstrate the overlap between the different types of writing.

In **descriptive writing**, you focus on a place or a person. When you write about a place, you naturally write about the people in a description of the scene. When you write about a person, you naturally write about a place or places associated with the person. **Focus** is the key word.

In **narrative writing**, you build an account of events that linked together. When you write a narrative, you control the selection and order of events. **Control** is the key word.

Writing is assessed at GCSE in two parts:
- content and organization
- sentence structure, punctuation and spelling.

Descriptive writing

What makes a good piece of descriptive writing?

1. The content will **engage and interest** the reader.

For example:

> **Describe a school sports day. Write the opening sentences of this piece of writing.**

It was a beautiful day and a primary school sports day was underway. The sun was glaring down upon the competitors and the spectators. A man was sitting on the grass in bright blue shorts and a bright yellow top. He had no hair and his head was already starting to show signs of sunburn. He was shouting encouragement at his son, 'Go Louis, go, go, go!!!!'...

Choose one of the following tasks and write a first sentence that would set you up for the rest of your description.

- **Write a description of a market at lunchtime.**
- **Describe the scene at a music concert when the main act first enters the stage.**
- **Describe the scene at an airport when families going on holiday are waiting at the check-in desk.**

EXAMINER'S TIP

- Some students probably try too hard with descriptive writing. They feel their descriptive skills have to be on show from the start. Relax, and start by writing some clear sentences that set you up.

2. The **organization** of the writing will be clear and orderly. Paragraphs will be used effectively with some structure and style.

For example:

The land began to appear through the clouds; we were approaching the harbour. It seemed that the seagulls were welcoming us back home and we couldn't wait to dock, so we started to scamper around, finding our belongings that were all about us from the long trip. The bell sounded and we knew it was only five minutes more.

EXAMINER'S TIP

- Students ask if they can use paragraphs in descriptive writing. Of course you can, and it's a good thing to do so. There are some natural breaks even within a short piece of writing, so take the opportunity to show that you know how and when to use them.

Write an opening paragraph for one of the following:
- **Imagine you are in a queue in the post office.**
- **You are on a bus that has been stopped at road works. Describe the scene.**

3. You need **detail** in a description, and you need thoughtful **vocabulary** to make the meaning of the description more precise.

For example, you could write:

A man on the shingle beach was reading the newspaper with the sun at his back.

or

A bronzed man facing away from the sun sat on the rough beach reading the Daily Mail.

The second is slightly more detailed, but it is easy to overdo it. Do we need 'bronzed'?

Using well-selected nouns and verbs can help to add detail:

The <u>rain fell</u> swiftly and soaked the old <u>woman striving</u> to <u>get home</u> with her overstuffed <u>shopping bags.</u>

Rewrite the following sentences adding extra detail. Think about changing the vocabulary to make each sentence more descriptive.

■ The house was small with a thatched roof in need of repair.

■ The children ran really fast across the sand because it was too hot for their small, bare feet.

■ The sky was full of big, grey clouds threatening a storm which started the minute I opened the door.

EXAMINER'S TIP

■ Don't feel that you need to add an adjective to every noun and an adverb to every verb in order to make your writing detailed. Also, avoid dropping impossibly long words into the description just to impress.

Examples of descriptive writing

Taking what you have learned into account, read the three extracts describing a dentist's waiting room below. How could you improve each of these pieces of writing? Make a list of corrections and suggestions for each one.

a) As I sat in the dentist's waiting room, I could see the wary faces of the patients. As the clock was ticking down to each of the patients' appointments, you could see their faces dropping to the floor as they hear the drill going in the dentist's room. The waiting room was a dull bland colour, there is nothing lively or entertaining for the patients, as the reception employee calls up the next patient to go to the dentist's room you could feel the fear going through his mind...

b) "Cough, cough," a man sat in the corner bellows out with a parade of killer coughing. Sat opposite a woman, holding a bloody rag over her mouth. A sudden wave of people covering their ears as they stood beneath the speaker blaring loudly. Calling the next patient. A smell of chemicals conquered the room...

c) As I was waiting for my booked appointment with the dentist, creaking chairs and a toddler playing with the toys that came from the toy box under the desk were the only activeness in the room. Vibration heard from through the walls and a slight moan representing the uncomfortable feeling the patient is going through...

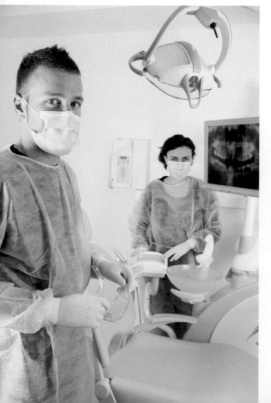

Narrative writing

How not to write a narrative

Narrative writing is about clear and meaningful communication to the reader. Remember, the key word is **control**, with **maturity** not far behind. You should avoidcreating a piece of 'genre writing' or unoriginal stories of horror, fantasy and war heroics. Writers of this kind of narrative are often re-living a film – badly – and forgetting that a good writer writes for the reader. Bad writers write to a formula – in other words, 'let's be predictable, let's feed off as many clichés as we can!' No, let's not!

> **Read the following extracts and list in detail the faults and failings of each one. (You are allowed to smile as you make the list!)**

a) I was sent on a dangerous mission that could end this war once and for all. I accepted reluctantly but I knew I was the only one who had a chance to infiltrate the city and take out the leader. It wasn't going to be easy as I would have to sneak in at night, and with the curfew active, guards were authorized to shoot on sight. I managed to get into the ventilation system of the government building. If I managed to get to the generator room and plant a bomb it could end it. By a stroke of luck there was a guard change. I took this opportunity, planted the bomb and escaped. When the explosion happened the flames licked the building and lit up the sky.

b) Shapes shoot through the door, seemingly hundreds of zombies file into the room. We shoot, they fall, more take their place. To my left I hear a scream, I turn to see Jebediah holding his chest as blood oozes between gashes. Something hits him in the dark, blood gushes and he lies still. I turn and run, grabbing Jermaine as I run; he quickly follows me. I fall over the colossus shape, I ignore the smell of burnt flesh and run...

To get it out of your system, create a corny paragraph of bad 'genre' writing – in fact, the 'badder' the better! Enjoy sharing them...

What makes a good piece of narrative writing?

1. The **plot** and the **characters** will be well-constructed and sustained.

For example, look at both of these stories entitled 'The Gift':

- My sixteenth birthday was today. Mum, Dad, Nan, Steve, Amy and Keith were all excited and told me to stay upstairs until they shouted at me to come down. What was going on? I had asked for many things but wasn't sure what money was available and had no idea what I was going to get.

- I had finally saved up enough money to buy it. I had worked every Saturday for the last six months and was now ready to go to Evergreens and pay for the small greenhouse my father had been desperate for. He had lost his job a year ago and was trying to make ends meet by growing vegetables and selling them at the local farmers' market in town.

EXAMINER'S TIP

■ Keep the plot manageable and keep the number of characters down to three or four only.

1. **Look at the first example and identify the problem with the plot and characters. Then rewrite the first few lines to make it more interesting and constructive.**
2. **Look at the second example and explain how you think the story could develop and what the brief few lines tell you about the main character of the story. Then write a few more sentences continuing the story.**

2. There will be a **good beginning** and an **appropriate ending**.

For example:

It was a balmy summer evening. We had lit the barbeque and the chicken was basting in the marinade waiting for the guests to arrive. Everyone seemed to be there, until we realized Matt hadn't yet turned up. Maybe he was late leaving work, so we called the mini-market. No answer, so possibly the delivery van was in the back waiting to be unloaded. We left it a couple of minutes and then kept calling. We decided to use ringback in the hope that we would soon know where he was and when we could expect him. Half an hour passed and then the phone shrilled loudly in the hall; Mum answered and we could hear her asking who was there. Was it Matt? She smiled so we thought everything was alright, but. . .

Write the openings and endings for the following titles:
- **A Night Out**
- **Living in the Past**
- **The Birthday Party**

EXAMINER'S TIP

■ You have plenty of time to think about the opening sentences. Openings can set up expectations for a story but above all clear, precise sentences set up expectations of quality and control. Think about the ending before you start. Don't spoil a good story with a hopeless ending.

3. The narrative is **purposeful** and **well-paced**.

For example, what information do you gather from the paragraph below about the house and the narrator's reasons for travelling?

I arrived at the small village of Bursford at the allocated time of 9am as I had promised. The driver was waiting, suited and booted and holding a sign with my name on it. He carried my luggage and informed me the drive to the hotel would be little more than half an hour, so I could settle myself. As we drove into the hotel, I was blown away by how big and imposing the building was and how grand the gardens were. I was now a little nervous as to how I was going to get through the next two days of testing and assessment in order to get the job I really wanted as Head Housekeeper.

> **Continue the following: 'He could resist everything except temptation, and this was very tempting...' and set some expectations and clues for the reader.**

EXAMINER'S TIP

- In a narrative of two or three pages, you have to be selective. Narratives that travel along a motorway stopping at every service station never reach the end of the journey. Selected snapshots, well signposted, are very important.

4. Paragraphs will be varied in length, with **links** and **connectives** keeping the story progressing.

For example:

Sat looking at the rippling water at Ullswater, I saw fleeting shadows of the small fish happily swimming in the clear blue water. The lake was vast with many small islands jutting out, scattered here and there.

An hour passed, and still I sat silently watching, and listening to the many sounds around me. I heard birds singing and calling to one another. If I listened hard enough, I could hear the faint voices of the hikers beginning their journey across to the next lake.

In the next glade, there was a family setting up their picnic. The smell of their food wafted over to me with various aromas of cakes and sausages awakening my stomach. They were laughing and enjoying the time spent together.

> Set up a piece of descriptive writing about a motorway service area by writing the opening sentences for three successive paragraphs.
> Do the same for a place you have visited and remember well. Set up the description with three key topic sentences for your paragraphs.

EXAMINER'S TIP

- Paragraphing is not rocket science. Before you develop the confidence for variation, begin with paragraphs of roughly equal length. Connectives can be associated words, or they can be the grammatical words and phrases that signal a change, e.g. 'One hour later...', 'In the next village...' or simply, 'However...'

5. Overall the **reader's interest is held**, perhaps by means of interesting devices, words, phrases and sentences.

For example:

- I never wanted to return to the place of my birth but an anonymous email sent to my personal address had captured my interest...
- Watching my small children allowing the sand to gather between their toes, feeling the grains moving around their feet, I suddenly became aware of tears welling...
- It was an empty tin can...

> Discuss the potential of each of the examples above. Write at least one or two sentences to continue each example.

EXAMINER'S TIP

- Examples of narrative devices are flashbacks and cliff-hangers, amongst others, but the best devices of all are well-chosen words and phrases, and crisp sentences, that are properly punctuated.

Examples of narrative writing

The following extracts are taken from narratives written by GCSE students. The first is the opening of an account of a personal experience. The second is also rooted in reality but it is a clear step towards fiction in its response to the simple title.

1

<u>My Bright Blue Plaster Cast</u>

It was a normal day for me at primary school. I woke up. Well that was a good thing! I had my normal everyday lessons. It was all fine.

The bell rang for lunch and I was excited because it was our turn to go on the climbing frame in the school playground. My group of friends met up with me at the play area so we could play a game. We all decided who was going to be on or not. The game was going great until I climbed up the ladder, ran across, slipped and fell off it. And then I felt my arm snap! The rush of pins of needles up my arm was excruciating and I was in agony.

People started to gather around me, and they were saying "keep still" and, "your arm isn't broken". I insisted I had broken my arm. My arm was still. I was too scared to move, I was in limbo. I did not know what to do next. . .

2

<u>A Knock on the Door</u>

Assertively, Sergeant Major Roberts gave three hard booms on the door. A petite woman very pretty yet seemingly stressed answered the door. The second she caught sight of the sergeant major her eyes flooded leaving a cascading waterfall down her face, "Is Private Jenkins in the building, madam?" barked Roberts in a stereotypically military manner, but by the time he had said that the lady had ran into her house leaving the door wide open.

The sergeant stepped into their domain and examined the entrance hall, scattered with toys and coats. He overheard Mr and Mrs Jenkins squabbling violently in another room. A shatter of glass left the house silent as Mr and Mrs Jenkins stepped into the hall.

Mr Jenkins gave his sergeant a crisp salute, the sergeant did not return the gesture and neglected to say at ease, he merely examined the private and thought to himself how ordinary his soldier looked in his 'civvies'.

"Private Jenkins," bellowed the sergeant with mock reassurance, "did you enjoy your time away from Her Majesty's royal armed forces, so much that you forgot to show up at Katterick's training ground?"

"Sir, no sir" barked Private Jenkins.

"I know soldier, I am not stupid" screamed the sergeant. "Did you think that we wouldn't realize your absence?"

"Sir, no, sir" he shrieked with a heavy note of guilt in his voice.

"You have been AWOL for two weeks now, Private, if it were up to me I would have you hung."

"Sir, permission to speak freely, sir".

"Denied" said the sergeant with a vicious smile on his face. "Unfortunately for me Private, I am not able to give you your punishment as I am only here to take you back". He surveyed the Private's guilt-ridden face and shouted: "You have five minutes soldier, to say goodbye and to grab your things. I will be waiting in the car. If you are even one second more I have twelve shiny little friends in my gun that might find you sooner than I do."

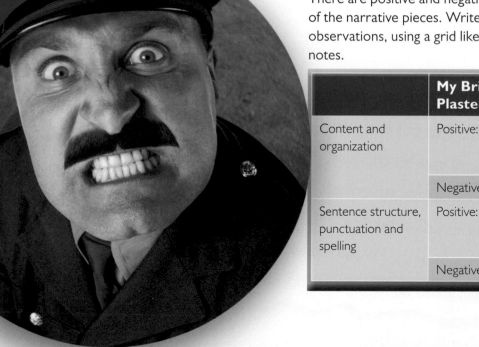

There are positive and negative things to be said about each of the narrative pieces. Write down your comments and observations, using a grid like the one below to organize your notes.

	My Bright Blue Plaster Cast	A Knock on the Door
Content and organization	Positive:	Positive:
	Negative:	Negative:
Sentence structure, punctuation and spelling	Positive:	Positive:
	Negative:	Negative:

Autobiography

Writing an autobiography is the process of remembering and retelling. It is written in the first person and tells the story of a person's life, or of an event in a person's life, from his or her perspective. A full autobiography is usually written when someone has lived for some time, so that they are able to look back at the context of their life when describing events, but everyone is able to write autobiographically about some of their memories.

Read the following piece of autobiographical writing by a GCSE student:

When I was younger, I would frequently go and stay with my grandparents, who lived in the quiet seaside town of St Bees in Cumbria. I remember once, when I was about five years old, my brother, father and I paid them a visit, we were to stay for the night and go home the next evening. As we arrived, my grandmother came out, cigarette in hand, and embraced me, hugging me tight, while almost singeing my elder brother's shirt with her cigarette. This was not uncommon, both my grandparents smoked about twenty a day, and would carelessly wave their cigarettes around, unintentionally jabbing anything that got in the way. As we entered the house, the smell of fresh baking wafted into our nostrils, shortly followed by my grandfather's smell of cigarettes and whisky.

My grandparents were how all grandparents should be: loving, caring and enjoying their retirements thoroughly. After this brief greeting, my brother and I assumed our usual position on the sofa, eyes fixated upon the television. Grandpa had Sky television, in the days when this was quite a rarity. Cartoon network was our channel of choice, watching around four hours of this per day, as well as taking a leisurely stroll on the beach with the dog, Meg, who was always happy to see us. Possibly because we would always feed her under the table, with our grandfather, it was our little secret, and my brother and I vowed never to tell it to anybody. After a traditional meal, which would always consist of meat and freshly picked vegetables from our grandfather's garden, always with potatoes and tomatoes, we would walk the dog along the pebble-ridden beach. My brother and I would roar with laughter as Meg would chase seagulls, never once succeeding to catch one.

After returning home, we once again assumed the position in front of the television, with a mug of hot cocoa, while munching on fresh cake and chocolate bars. Every day followed a very similar pattern. It would consist of television, being spoilt eating cakes and chocolates and walking the dog before returning home. One of my fondest memories was when my dear grandpa complained furiously that I never ate the white of my egg. I could never understand why, until recently my father explained that as a child of the war, he could never waste food. After breakfast, my grandmother would always join us watching television, with yet another cigarette, and a cup of coffee, happy to just watch her beloved grandchildren whom she rarely saw, simply watch television. Occasionally we would have a simple conversation, which would always revolve around her utter adoration of the family. When it was finally time to go home, my grandpa would always have a treat for us to part with, whether it was a packet of crisps, a chocolate bar, or a can of 'pop', which he would refer to it as, much to my brother's and my amusement.

This visit may seem rather insignificant, however, this was the last time my brother and I ever saw our grandma, the last time we smelt her perfume that all grandmothers seem to wear, the last time she ever told us she loved us. I will always remember that weekend we stayed at their small, quiet, sea-view bungalow.

The above piece is not word-perfect — it shows lapses of control in punctuation and grammar — but it is a beautifully sensitive and affectionate piece of writing. The ending is genuinely sad, despite it being a low-key, undramatic revelation of the death of the grandmother.

First-person and third-person writing

A first-person piece of writing, often a narrative, is written from the perspective of **I** or **we** (grammatical first person). The narrator is therefore firmly in the story.

A third-person piece of writing is written from a more detached point of view. The writer is generally outside the immediate action, looking in. It is written from the perspective of **he**, **she** or **they** (grammatical third person).

As with narrative writing, descriptive writing can also be written from a first-person or a third-person perspective, but it is not so easy to keep in focus when writing a first-person description. First-person writing can naturally drift towards narrative writing. The following chart may help:

	First person	Third person
Descriptive writing	In the scene with restricted view. Observations and feelings mixed.	Clear view and possible to zoom in and out.
Narrative writing	Story told from point of view of **I**. Right in the action, but can't see everything.	Story from point of view of **he** or **she**. Probably outside the action, but can see everything.

Read the piece of narrative writing below:

The Dare

My friend and I pose challenges to one another on a daily basis. Whether it be something stupid like setting off fireworks on school grounds, or spitting off a bridge.

Today was my time to play the fool. I stared over that open canyon, a swirl of wind blowing endlessly around my ankles; the relentless sound of engines gushing out smog. Describing the motorway as a canyon may be overdramatic, but at this time, I felt I would be safer walking on a tight rope between two ten-storey buildings. I climbed slowly up the steel cage; it shook violently, as it attempted to knock me off. I could hear the noise of sounding horns, and angry, jeering cries from the bridge parallel to the sign. I was fully aware of how much trouble I would be in, but the pressing matter at hand was walking across the narrow platform.

I finally reached the top, and suddenly, everything fell silent, the cars began to slow down. I stood perfectly still, every muscle in my body had cramped up, as if it was locked stiff. I forced one step forward, feeling the slow flowing traffic had given me more confidence and immediately a rush of sound and a flurry of speeding trucks brought me back to reality and I retracted my foot instantly.

Now imagine this had been written as a third-person narrative. The opening sentence might be something like: 'Taylor and Nick posed challenges to one another…' The second paragraph could begin: 'Today was Nick's turn to play the fool'.

Re-write the third and final paragraph as a third-person narrative. Consider the obvious differences between the two. Does it matter? Which do you prefer for this particular story? What would be your preferred ending for each of the two versions?

Now read this piece of descriptive writing, composed from a third-person, 'outsider' point of view:

It is the first day of the new year at a school. This is the scene at the beginning of the day.
    After six weeks of a melancholy grey colour, the school car-park now resembles a rainbow, as blue Golfs, red Hondas and, in one case, a silver Jaguar line up and are emptied of their living content. Teachers, old and young, exit their cars and begin a mad dash to their classrooms, desperate not to have to be the one that tells the huge Year Elevens to stop booting their football against the nearest classroom door. A few yards away from the gang of muscular boys and their football is a group of six or seven girls, all giggling and pointing fingers at the boys. A fair distance away from this, a sweet wrapper bounces across the playground floor like tumbleweed, only to be picked up by the headmaster, who sweeps the playground with his eyes, trying to root out the student that may have dropped it. Unable to do so, he walks over to the nearest bin to deposit it, only to find the smallest Year Seven tucked away at the bottom. The bell rings for the first time in a month and a half, and the playground empties. Another year begins.

Try to rewrite the description from a first person point of view. (In this particular case, it is quite difficult, because the writer would have to be a pupil or teacher and would be drawn to others in a different way. Only the boy in the bin would have a fresh perspective, and he might not see a great deal from where he is!)

What makes a good, accurate piece of English writing?

1. **The sentences are varied and controlled**. Short sentences can be used to add impact. Make sure that longer sentences end before they run away loosely.
2. **Accurate punctuation** is used to vary pace, clarify meaning, and create deliberate effects: Get your full stops right first and remember commas are not substitutes for full stops.
3. **Virtually all spelling**, including that of complex irregular words, is correct.

HELP!

EXAMINER'S TIP

- There is some tolerance of incorrect spellings of difficult words, and even the odd slip in a common word, but generally you must be on top of the standard rules about plurals, consonants and vowels. Homophones (sound-alike words) and other very frequently used words need to be correct!

4. **Grammar** is used confidently and purposefully. Use Standard written English: You don't have to be posh, just proper!

Here is an imaginative, focused, controlled piece of writing that shows all of the above.

Locked In

Trapped. Locked in, enclosed, imprisoned, unable to escape, denied freedom. I try the door again, rattling the orange handle in annoyance. It seems I entered this port-a-loo of no return, and somehow locked the door from the outside, clever me. I try the door again with more force but less aggression. I can hear people outside still, the game is just about to start, I consider calling for help, but the thought of being 'the port-a-loo guy' is unbearable. No, I am going to get out of this myself.

Another ten minutes pass, still stuck like a coin in a miser's wallet. I am fervently hoping that someone will need to use this toilet, so they'll get me out, but it is still set to 'ENGAGED' and the little catch to change it is as immovable as a beached whale, despite being half an inch thick. I take stock of my surroundings, or shall I say, surrounding. Seven feet from floor to roof, and three feet wide by three feet deep. Like a coffin. A big, fluorescent orange coffin. There is a moulded plastic sink (with no tap) and a hand sanitizer on the wall, informing me that 99% of germs can be killed by washing regularly. I wonder what percentage of people are killed by port-a-loo? I don't want to be a statistic but I'm not feeling optimistic *about escape either. Running my hands along the wall, feeling the hard, smooth plastic, I finally realize the smell wafting up. The less said about it, the better, but after 20 minutes of exposure I am starting to feel light-headed. Realizing that any dignity I may have remaining would be forfeited if I died from methane inhalation, I decide to call for help. It is at this point that I realize everyone has gone.*

This should sharpen my resolve to explore; instead, I begin to look for a scrap of paper on which to record my will and final testament...

Controlled Assessment Practice – English Language

1. Write a page of **description** on ONE of the topics listed.
   - Describe a place you know well.
   - Describe a place that needs to be protected for the future.

2. Choose one of the following options and write a **narrative** of two to three sides.
   - My moment of triumph.
   - Coming home.
   - Write about an incident that taught you a valuable lesson.

Controlled Assessment Practice – English

Plan and write three paragraphs of **first-person narrative writing** on one of the topics listed below.
- Write about a time when you volunteered for something.
- Write about an occasion when you appeared on stage.

Plan and write three paragraphs of **third-person narrative writing** on one of the topics listed below.
- Liam meeting Lucy's parents for the first time.
- Ashley's ghostly experience.

How is writing assessed at GCSE?

Assess your writing using the checklist below to see where improvements could be made.

CONTENT AND ORGANIZATION – DESCRIPTIVE WRITING

Content: is it…
- ❑ okay, but patchy?
- ❑ relevant and quite interesting?
- ❑ relevant, makes good sense, and keeps the reader's interest?
- ❑ really well-judged, sustained and pertinent, firmly engaging the reader's interest?

Organization: is the writing…
- ❑ partly organized?
- ❑ mostly organized?
- ❑ properly organized?
- ❑ really skillfully and stylishly constructed?

Paragraphs: are they…
- ❑ used?
- ❑ logically ordered and sequenced?
- ❑ used consciously to structure the writing?
- ❑ effective in length and structure to control detail and progression?

Detail: is there…
- ❑ selection of detail but often at a general level?
- ❑ some attempt to focus on detail?
- ❑ some well-organized detail within and between paragraphs?
- ❑ quality detailed content within and between paragraphs?

Vocabulary: is there…
- ❑ a limited range with little variation of word choice?
- ❑ some range, occasionally selected to create effects?
- ❑ a range of vocabulary selected to create effects or convey precise meaning?
- ❑ a wide range of well-judged, ambitious vocabulary?

CONTENT AND ORGANIZATION – NARRATIVE WRITING

Plot and characterization: is there…
- [ ] a basic sense of plot and characters?
- [ ] some control of plot and characters?
- [ ] overall control of plot and characters?
- [ ] a well-constructed plot and developed characters?

Beginnings and endings: is there…
- [ ] a loose sense of a beginning and ending?
- [ ] a suitable beginning and an intended conclusion?
- [ ] a deliberate opening and a satisfactory, meaningful ending?
- [ ] an arresting opening and a thoughtful ending?

Narrative purpose: is it…
- [ ] a simple, basic piece of writing?
- [ ] a narrative with some conscious construction?
- [ ] an organized and purposefully sequenced story?
- [ ] a well-paced, deliberately organized and sequenced narrative?

Cohesion: is there…
- [ ] some simple continuity in the writing?
- [ ] logical connections throughout the narrative?
- [ ] detailed content, well-organized within and between paragraphs?
- [ ] cohesion reinforced by the use of text connectives and other linking devices?

Paragraphs: are they …
- [ ] used?
- [ ] logically ordered and sequenced?
- [ ] used consciously to structure the writing?
- [ ] effective in length and structure to control detail and progression?

Devices: are there…
- [ ] some words deliberately chosen?
- [ ] some deliberate choice of vocabulary and a variety of sentence lengths?
- [ ] some skills (devices) to achieve particular effects?
- [ ] skills (devices) used consciously and effectively to achieve particular effects?

Overall and reader's interest: is the writing…
- [ ] coherent enough to follow and able to briefly engage the reader?
- [ ] clear and credible and developed to engage the reader's interest?
- [ ] controlled, coherent and shaped, with good pace and detail?
- [ ] developed with originality and imagination; confident and assured?

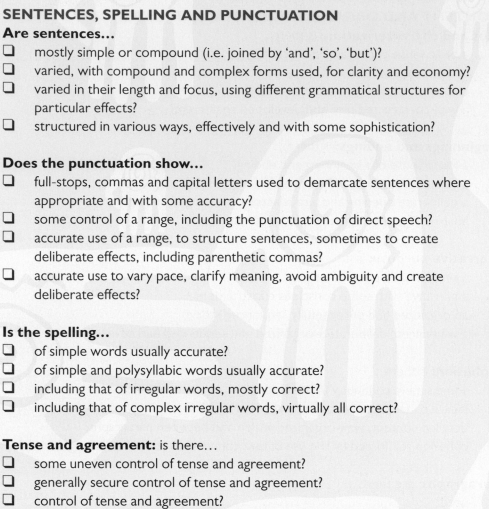

SENTENCES, SPELLING AND PUNCTUATION

Are sentences...
- ❑ mostly simple or compound (i.e. joined by 'and', 'so', 'but')?
- ❑ varied, with compound and complex forms used, for clarity and economy?
- ❑ varied in their length and focus, using different grammatical structures for particular effects?
- ❑ structured in various ways, effectively and with some sophistication?

Does the punctuation show...
- ❑ full-stops, commas and capital letters used to demarcate sentences where appropriate and with some accuracy?
- ❑ some control of a range, including the punctuation of direct speech?
- ❑ accurate use of a range, to structure sentences, sometimes to create deliberate effects, including parenthetic commas?
- ❑ accurate use to vary pace, clarify meaning, avoid ambiguity and create deliberate effects?

Is the spelling...
- ❑ of simple words usually accurate?
- ❑ of simple and polysyllabic words usually accurate?
- ❑ including that of irregular words, mostly correct?
- ❑ including that of complex irregular words, virtually all correct?

Tense and agreement: is there...
- ❑ some uneven control of tense and agreement?
- ❑ generally secure control of tense and agreement?
- ❑ control of tense and agreement?
- ❑ change in tense and is this used confidently and purposefully?

Preparing for Controlled Assessment

Here are the relevant details from the GCSE specifications for this part of the assessment, including the Assessment Objectives for each specification (these are the skills you are trying to show to gain marks and grades).

 GCSE ENGLISH LANGUAGE UNIT 3: Literary Reading and Creative Writing

Using language: creative writing (15%)

Controlled Assessment

You will need to write **one** piece of descriptive writing and **one** piece of narrative/expressive writing drawn from tasks supplied by WJEC.

AO4 Writing

● Write to communicate clearly, effectively and imaginatively, using and adapting forms and selecting vocabulary appropriate to task and purpose in ways which engage the reader.

- Organize information and ideas into structured and sequenced sentences, paragraphs and whole texts, using a variety of linguistic and structural features to support cohesion and overall coherence.
- Use a range of sentence structures for clarity, purpose and effect, with accurate punctuation and spelling.

GCSE ENGLISH UNIT 3: English in the World of the Imagination

Writing: open writing (20%), first and third person narrative

Controlled Assessment

You will need to write **one** piece of first person and **one** piece of third person narrative writing drawn from tasks supplied by WJEC.

AO3 Writing

- Write clearly, effectively and imaginatively, using and adapting forms and selecting vocabulary appropriate to task and purpose in ways which engage the reader.
- Organize information and ideas into structured and sequenced sentences, paragraphs and whole texts, using a variety of linguistic and structural features to support cohesion and overall coherence.
- Use a range of sentence structures for clarity, purpose and effect, with accurate punctuation and spelling.

How to prepare for the Controlled Assessment tasks

Before the day

Think about it: Descriptive Writing

Descriptive writing requires you to write about a place or a person. Often when you are asked to write about a particular place, you will naturally include people in your description of the place. The key thing to remember is to focus on the scene or the character portrait; You should not tell a story.

So, you need to be focused and you also need to be a little bit individual. Or, to put it another away, you need to avoid being general. For example, in a crowded school dining room, it is likely that some people might be shouting and some might be eating quietly, so do not write 'Everybody was shouting'.

Be realistic in your description – how often do you hear patients screaming out in pain when you visit the dentist? Answer: never! So don't write 'The patient was screaming…'!

Any description is **subjective**; in other words, it is the writer's own view of a scene. It is possible to **highlight** certain features, and also to **understate** or 'play down' others. Each choice of a word can be crucial; a single pupil could be described as 'confident', 'cheeky', 'unruly', or 'outspoken', each of them offering a connotation or suggested meaning.

Try to form a picture in your head and then bring the scene to life.

Think about it: Narrative/expressive writing
Writing a story or a narrative is a test of maturity, and if you write something that is silly and childish, you will not get a high mark. It may be artificial to ask you to write a story in a Controlled Assessment, but your writing skills are being examined as well, under pressure.

Don't knock story-telling – we all do it every day of our lives. From ancient history to up-to-the-minute gossip, story-telling keeps the world going round.

Genre fiction is the name given to types of novel that can be easily categorized; for example, romance, horror, science-fiction, mystery or fantasy. On the whole, these kinds of writing do not work well under pressure because they so often depend on complicated plots.

In contrast, **autobiographical** and **travel writing** do work well for GCSE candidates. With autobiography, there is opportunity to use **personal history** and refer to **public events**, as well to experiment with the process of remembering. Remember that even in the best writing, mystery and suspense can come from ordinary, everyday events.

Travel writing is less common, but students write well about places they have experienced and people they have met. Make sure, however, that you do not describe at length the outward journey to a holiday destination and then run out of time! Put yourself in the place straightaway and create a clear **sense of place**.

Think your writing through to the end before you start.

The brief: Descriptive writing
This requires a 'picture in words'. It does not call for the action of a story, but you do need some variety of observation, some movement, some individuality for a successful piece of writing. From the first word to the last, stay with the place you are describing. Description is a set of carefully selected and weighed features, blended together.

Hold the features in your head:
Use a grid like the one on the right to organize your thoughts.

People – as individuals	
Names – of places and items	
Dialogue – brief snatches	
Nouns/verbs – for precision	
The weather – part of the outdoors	
Movement – part of a scene	
Senses – some, not all	

The brief: Narrative/expressive writing

People's lives are narratives and make history. We tell stories every day of our lives. Storytelling keeps the world going round. Creating an interesting narrative can be seen as a set of choices and steps.

Hold the steps in your head:

Use a grid like the one below to help you plan your work.

Opening	
A situation that develops	
A complication	
A crisis	
A resolution (or ending)	

On the day

- Do not try to memorize a prepared piece of work.
- Do not try to write out everything twice.
- Above all, make sure you know more or less how and where your writing is going to end.
- Pay some important attention to the beginning of each piece of writing.
- Control the steps along the way.

Proofreading your work

Last but certainly not least, it is important that you can quickly read through your work and identify inaccuracies. Correct mistakes in spelling, punctuation and grammar and look for improperly formed sentences and omitted words.

- Proofread your spelling.
- Proofread your punctuation.
- Proofread your grammar.

FOCUS ON THE EXAM   LA UNIT 2   E UNIT 2

GCSE English Language Unit 2

GCSE English Unit 2

In this paper, you will write two pieces of transactional writing which will be worth 20 marks each. You will be able to write for a range of audiences and purposes, adapting style to form and to suit real-life contexts.

Transactional writing

Transactional writing is 'real-life' writing where there exists a clear relationship between the writer and the reader. This form of writing can involve discussing issues and giving opinions.

The key questions to ask when creating a piece of transactional writing are:

- What is the purpose? (i.e. the reason for the task)
- Who is the audience? (i.e. the person or people reading it)
- What is the format? (i.e. the shape and layout of the writing)

In this chapter you will develop skills and practise writing tasks that require you to combine information and ideas. You will be set 'real-life' tasks and you will learn how to improve your writing under pressure - both for the exam and for some of the realities of adult life.

Types of text

Here are some examples of the types of text you may be asked to write in your exam:

leaflets   reports   speeches   reviews   formal letters   articles

Reports

Reports are written in an impersonal style. They may be written by an individual but they often represent the viewpoints of a number of people. Reports are usually directed at an official leader of an organization; for instance, the chairperson of a governing body.

Features of reports:
- report heading (e.g. 'Report on the eating habits of school children')
- the recipient of the report (e.g. 'To The Board of Governors')
- the sender of the report (e.g. 'From a representative from Catering')
- an introduction
- subheadings (e.g. 'Main Course', 'Dessert', 'Fruit and Vegetables')
- impersonal style (e.g. avoid the use of 'I' – 'The department has decided...')
- bullet points
- conclusions/recommendations (i.e. suggestions for future action).

Letters

Letter writing is important, even in these days of emails and mobile phones. Formal letters are still used in business and letters from readers are still frequently printed in newspapers. Informal letters can be sent by snail-mail or e-mail, and should be written in controlled, coherent and organized English.

Features of formal letters:
- your address as the sender goes in the top right-hand corner
- receiver's name and address on the left-hand side*
- the correct opening (Dear Sir/Madam, Dear Mr Smith, Dear Editor)
- a suitable, precise opening sentence; avoid opening with 'I am writing to you...'
- a number of well-developed paragraphs
- a firm summing-up of the purpose of the letter
- avoidance of shortened forms (e.g. 'I'm', 'don't', 'won't', etc.)*
- use of appropriate vocabulary
- suitable and appropriate signing off (e.g. 'Yours faithfully' with 'Dear Sir')*.

NB Items marked with asterisks (*) do not apply to informal letters

EXAMINER'S TIP

- Some students probably try too hard with descriptive writing. They feel their descriptive skills have to be on show from the start. Relax, and start by writing some straightforward sentences that will help you to begin your writing clearly.

Articles

An article is a piece of writing included in a newspaper or magazine. It is not the headline news, but a discussion of a topical issue, often from a particular point of view.

Features of articles:
- a lively opening providing an idea, example or anecdote to interest the reader
- a clearly-argued position on the topic being discussed
- a clear variation in sentence lengths, showing impact, subtlety and clarity
- a consideration of the opposing views
- integration of supporting evidence and examples
- a conclusion or ending that attempts to take the argument forward.

Reviews

Reviews are used to communicate a personal opinion about things such as programmes, films, books or performances. The aim of the review is to persuade the reader to adopt the same opinion of the subject as the reviewer.

Reviews should:
- stimulate an interest in whatever you are reviewing
- show respect even if the review is negative
- steer the reader to your point of view
- avoid reiterating the plot
- avoid writing an English Literature essay, if doing a book review
- give the important details, such as key people involved, venue of performance, etc.
- be aimed at the intelligent non-expert.

Speeches

A speech can be formal or informal, depending upon the audience. However, even an informal 'speech' such as a contribution to a phone-in should be in Standard English.

Guidlines for speeches:
●   In most cases, a speech should begin without fuss.
●   Write in full sentences because you are arguing a case.
●   Notes are not enough – use paragraphs to create a sense of order.
●   Usually, you will argue from a personal point of view.

Leaflets

Leaflets are short promotional texts designed to attract the interest of people and inform them about topics or goods.

Features of leaflets:
●   a heading and subheadings
●   bullet-points (but do not overdo them)
●   columns (although you do not have to do this)

You may wish to include an image in your leaflet. Do not draw the image – just draw a box to show where the image would go.

> **Draw a logo for each of these types of text. Label each logo with key words that relate to the features of that text type.**

Writing under pressure

In the exam, you will have one hour to complete your transactional writing tasks. You need to learn how to plan, write and proofread your work effectively under pressure.

Context

Sometimes the situation surrounding the task will be given to you in the exam, but sometimes you will have to create the context.

A local hotel/restaurant is advertising for part-time staff. You decide to apply.

Write your letter of application.

The quality of your writing is more important than its length. You should write about one to two pages in your answer book.

In the task above the context is easy to imagine, but you still need to 'invent' the name of the hotel or restaurant and you also need to visualize the place. However, in some tasks you might be given extra details. Ensure you read the question carefully to determine what is being asked of you.

In the next task, you have more work to do in contextualising your writing.

Imagine you have a friend or relative who is considering going to live abroad.

Write a letter giving your opinions.

Some questions you might ask in this case are:
- Who is going to live abroad?
- Where are they going?
- Why are they going?
- Is it a permanent move?
- What are your views on their decision?

The following response might give the examiner a laugh, but it is an example of how **not** to do it.

> Dear Wayne,
>
> I hear you are thinking of moving abroad. Don't do it. You know you don't like foreigners and you don't like their food. And you'll have trouble with the language. You can't even speak English.
>
> Alex

Write a response to one of the above tasks. Use between one and two sides of A4 paper.

Content

In the exam, you must have something of substance and meaning to write about, whatever the task. Look at the task and example response below.

> **Write an article for your local newspaper about a place in the community that deserves to be respected, protected, and possibly improved.**

The Nature Reserve is an area of deciduous woodland owned by the Forestry Commission but managed by the RSPB. It is home to many rare species of birds, including the pied flycatcher, and it has some old oak trees dating back to Elizabethan times. In summer the ponds contain many damselflies and dragonflies, frogs and other animals and it is a lovely peaceful place.

The problem is that some people like to put fish in the ponds. This may seem a good idea, but fish will eat the dragonfly larvae, damselfly larvae and tadpoles as food, which in turn affects wildlife further up the food chain, unbalancing the whole ecosystem around the pond. The staff on the reserve have been trying to catch all the fish in the pond to get rid of them, but as more are being put in, it is an impossible task.

If anyone knows someone who is doing this, please contact the reserve's warden so that the wildlife in this beautiful pond can be saved.

The writing above shares detailed information with the reader. The student has grabbed the opportunity to choose a place in the community that he or she knows about. The choice is good, the information is detailed and the idea is clear, although the writing could be more persuasive.

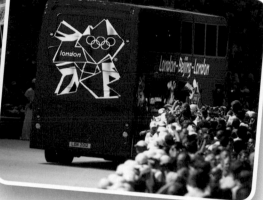

Writing process

In an examination you need to think quickly, but do not neglect your planning. Look at the example tasks below.

A

Write a speech to your class **FOR** or **AGAINST** being a vegetarian.

B

Write a letter to a national broadsheet newspaper **FOR** or **AGAINST** the use of Facebook in schools.

C

Write an article for your local newspaper **FOR** or **AGAINST** the UK bidding for showpiece world sporting events like the Olympics or the rugby or football World Cup.

In the exam, you will not have a choice of tasks, but it is worth putting these three tasks alongside one another to show the importance of **positioning** in the writing process. Positioning simply means ensuring that you start in the right place!

All of the three tasks require opinion, argument and persuasion... and some general knowledge (you don't have to be an expert!).

Each of them requires you to have a clear view – For or Against. You do not write an article, speech or letter if you are half-hearted about something. It is important though to understand the counter-arguments.

EXAMINER'S TIP

- Remember you need to open with a clear, coherent sentence, not a confused, complicated statement of theory.

Don't forget the format requirements of the type of writing you are undertaking. A speech requires a sense of appropriate spoken English. (For example: 'Most people here know that I'm a vegetarian, and some of them think I'm completely mad.'), while an article requires a headline, and a letter requires at least one address, a date, and a salutation (For example: 'Dear...').

In each of the tasks on the previous page, you need to have a sense of the **purpose**, or the reason for writing. You may need to think about that and work at it. Also note your audience: the people that you are 'speaking' to. You need to keep that in mind, in order to keep the focus.

Look again at the tasks on the previous page.

Task A

Why would you speak to the class about eating meat or not eating meat? What are the issues of vegetarianism? What do young people understand or misunderstand about the topic? Could it be a lively topic of debate where people disagree passionately? Could some people be interested in the topic, but a little bit short of knowledge?

Task B

What are the key points you want to get across? What issues have there been surrounding the use of Facebook? Are you basing your opinion on personal experience? How can it be dangerous? Are there any educational benefits? How might it be used? To contact strangers? To keep in touch with friends and family? What about information available on profiles and definitions of friendships?

Task C

What are your opinions on holding these sporting events in this country? How would you feel if you lived in the area where the event will take place? What do you want to get across in your letter? Are you interested in sports or football? Will it increase employment or revenue in the area? What additional information would be useful to back up your point of view? Would it increase traffic? Who would benefit? What about concerns for security?

When writing, you should clarify your position. You are entitled to have your doubts and contradicting opinions, but you need to sort them out into a well-reasoned argument. Your argument will become stronger, not weaker, if you can weigh up the merits of an opposing argument. Sometimes you can be assertive; sometimes it is beneficial to be cautious and measured.

Composing

In your writing, you need to use paragraphs and clear, coherent sentences.

Formal reports and letters can be structured logically using headings, subheadings and bullet points. Consider the tasks below:

The Governors of your school or college are interested in the views of pupils/students. They have asked you to write a report, pointing out the strengths and weaknesses of your school or college.

Continue the report below, writing at least three or four sentences under each subheading. Then complete the report with final recommendations, in the form of clear bullet points. The style of writing (formal) is set by the opening.

REPORT FROM A SENIOR STUDENT ON   _____
SCHOOL/COLLEGE
SUBMITTED TO THE GOVERNING BODY ON   _____ (date)
The following report, as requested by the governors, offers the considered views of representatives of senior students.
<u>Facilities and equipment</u>
<u>Buildings</u>
<u>Range of subjects</u>
<u>Out-of-school activities</u>
<u>Conclusions and recommendations</u>

B Write an anti-smoking leaflet aimed at young people.

Continue the leaflet below, writing at least three or four sentences under each subheading. Then complete the leaflet with a strong, persuasive finish, using bullet points if you wish. The style of writing (informal) is set by the opening.

GREAT REASONS TO STOP SMOKING!
Do you want to stop smoking? Do you want to improve your life? Then read on!
1. BETTER HEALTH: _____
2. BETTER FITNESS: _____
3. MORE MONEY: _____
4. CLEANER HOUSE AND CLOTHES: _____

In other tasks, subheadings and bullet points are not required. Construct your answer by:
1. thinking and planning paragraphs coherently.
2. weaving sentences together cohesively.

This means, in simple terms, knowing where you are heading and steering yourself there smoothly. Here are two skilful samples of writing:

C Write an article discussing the future of printed books in the computer age.

Are books a thing of the past?

It is true that we are living in the age of computers. Everything we do is either affected or reflected by these seemingly wondrous machines with their 'intelligent' technological brains. Yet, do we see the advancement of computers as the demise of books?

Books have been around for centuries. From the Bible to the classics to Winnie the Pooh, everyone has their favourite. Why do we place such emotional value on books? I think that even though books are not alive, it is their ability to make another place and time come alive to us that makes them so special.

Books are portable - wherever you may go, you can have a book with you, be it in the starry beyond of space or the inky depths of the ocean. These amazing collections of words on paper allow us to travel in our minds; through books we are offered a temporary escape to another world.

D

Write an article for a teenage magazine promoting a serious interest in a particular sport, either for participants or spectators.

Rhythmic gymnastics - you heard it here first!

Pain is one of the facts of life, like death, except you have to deal with it again and again. It is not a type of behaviour, but learning to deal with pain positively is a life skill that should be taught. Rhythmic Gymnastics can teach you this. To quote my coach - "I want a gymnast who cries." She does not mean this literally - what she means is that she wants us to work as hard as we can, beyond when our muscles are screaming with pain, until they collapse, until our teeth are gritted as we sit in over-splits or try to backbend to contortionist proportions. You do not hear our gym full of complaints of all our injuries and pains - they are mentioned and sympathy is given, but that is it...

...To conclude, I believe that to be a rhythmic gymnast you need to be an all-round athlete: as flexible as a contortionist, as strong as an artistic gymnast (leaps and balances), as graceful as a ballerina, and with the hand-to-eye co-ordination of a juggler. You need extreme fitness, self-control, commitment, ambition, endurance, proctoring skills, pain-handling, pursuit of perfection, and the ability to get back up again if you fall. It teaches you team spirit, and how to work in a group with others relying on your every move, and how to achieve the impossible. Yes, Rhythmic Gymnastics is the all-time best sport.

Now write an article for a magazine aimed at teenagers about a particular interest or sport. Write it in four paragraphs, with three or four sentences per paragraph.

Writing with accuracy: spelling and grammar

Poor spelling and grammar blights a lot of writing at GCSE. In many cases it is down to carelessness, with sloppy habits resulting in errors that would not have been made in primary school.

You must take stock of your own performance in these basic skills. You need to get organized to improve weaknesses that you do not want to take forward into an exam. Although revising the following technical terms will not guarantee an improvement, it should make you more aware of the key issues surrounding spelling, grammar and punctuation.

Spelling

- What are **homophones**? Do you have a weakness in this area?
  Look closely at: 'There were too few people present so they were not allowed to run their meeting.'

- How does an understanding of **syllables** help your spelling? What are polysyllabic spellings?
  Look closely at: 'It was an interesting decision, causing an elaborate consultation.'

- What different rules for **plurals** do you know?
  Look closely at: 'Women attend football matches in large numbers these days.'

- Is your knowledge of **vowel sounds** and spellings accurate?
  Look closely at: 'The release of the band's new album gave fans a great sense of relief and pleasure.'

- Is your spelling of **double consonants and consonant clusters** reliable?
  Look closely at: 'Currently, it is common for traffic in holiday resorts in the middle of summer to be excessive. The transport problems in this country would be solved by investment in the rail industry.'

- What are **prefixes and suffixes**? How might knowledge of them help your spelling and vocabulary?
  Look closely at: 'It was impossible to untangle the unbelievable regulation immediately.'

- Are you in command of words with **silent letters**, especially those that begin with them?
  Look closely at: 'There was no doubt that he knew what a debt he owed to his ghost writer.'

Find all of the spelling and grammar errors in the text below.

Citty where on there worse loosing run of the seasen, so it were a releif to come thorough a dificult fixtuere on Wensday nite agianst Untied with a drawer.

Grammar

- Do you know the definition of a **simple sentence**, a **compound sentence** and a **complex sentence**?

  Look closely at: 'The sun was rising over the hills. He drank his tea and ate his snap. When he had finished eating, he moved on towards the town. Walking down the road…'

- What do you know about **passive** constructions and the passive voice?

  Look closely at: 'A wonderful time was had by them.'

- Do you know how to write **reported** or **indirect speech**?

  Look closely at: 'Devon said it had been the proudest moment of his life.'

- What different kinds of **nouns** are there?

  Look closely at: 'Last Monday the delivery of flowers gave Nancy a great surprise.'

- **Adjectives** and **adverbs** describe nouns and verbs, but what do you know about **comparatives** and **superlatives**?

  Look closely at: 'She claimed she was happier than before, but she seemed more stressed than ever. She was further in trouble financially, because her most elderly dependant was expensive to keep.'

- There are **regular and irregular verbs** (generally understood by native speakers because of common usage), but what are **modals** and **auxiliary verbs**?

  Look closely at: 'Cinderella, you shall go to the ball when you have finished your chores, but you must be back at twelve o'clock.'

- Are you confident about your understanding of **verb tenses**?

  Look closely at: 'He had had a difficult time, but after his operation he was a new man.'

- Do you know for sure what **prepositions** are?

  Look closely at: 'On the table lay the contract for the new house. Unfortunately, it was beyond his means so he refrained from signing it.'

- What different kinds of **pronouns** are there?

  Look closely at: 'I gave Jack my phone number and he gave me his.'

- What different **conjunctions** do you know?

  Look closely at: 'Although she was tired, she carried on because she had paid for the trip.'

Writing with style: variation of punctuation and sentence structure

Writers do not always give sufficient attention to sentence construction and control of punctuation. There are different styles of writing, but style itself is precise writing with well-judged word choices and sentence variety, chosen for the occasion.

Like a lot of the issues raised in this chapter, it is a question of raising your awareness and taking control of what you write down.

> **In the following short passage, replace each of the oblique lines with either a full-stop (and a capital letter) or a comma. Then write a paragraph of your own on the subject matter of image, fashion or celebrities.**

For some people / controlling what they eat becomes a way for them to feel they have control over their lives / if they can control how their bodies look by what food they eat / then they think their lives will be in order too / society's obsession with healthy eating is just a sign of the times / appearance is everything / if your body is in shape / people will like you and respect you for being in such fine form / celebrities who lose their baby weight in six weeks by only eating lettuce are admired / while the ones who take a few months to lose it are ridiculed by the press.

> **In the following passage, the commas are supplied, but you must decide where full-stops and capital letters are needed. Then write a paragraph of your own on healthy eating.**

Tips on Healthy Eating

Healthy eating is easily accomplished if you follow a few simple rules fruit and vegetables are bursting with vitamins that could help you considerably if you aim to eat five types per day, then you will be fighting fit in no time at all you should also try to exercise about three times per week, which is a very small price to pay for your life if you are concerned that you won't stick to a chocolate free diet, then do not worry, as that is precisely why diets are formed if you balance your eating, then a few treats like biscuits and cakes will not stop you from achieving your goal.

Commas, as well as full-stops (and capital letters), are needed in the following short piece. Decide where the punctuation should go and then write your own paragraph 'in tribute' to Michael Jackson.

The King of Pop as he was famously known possessed humanitarian qualities most musicians don't have he had a good caring heart often not associated with people who have a string of zeros in their bank accounts the late Mr Jackson donated to charity organizations all over the world he didn't like the thought of destitute children with empty stomachs children who barely had enough clothes to shield from either the scorching sun or the cold night air

Look closely at the first point of the three-point plan on saving energy below. Then, complete the other two short sections using imaginative ideas and careful punctuation.

<u>Saving energy</u> <u>A Fantastic Three-Point Plan</u>
1. <u>Lights:</u> Do you leave lights on during the day or when you are not using a room? If so, then this is one of the simplest ways to prevent energy waste. Firstly, you could use extra-efficient, energy-saving light bulbs. Then, all you have to do is remember to <u>switch them off</u> when you leave!
2. <u>Re-cycling</u>
3. <u>Transport</u>

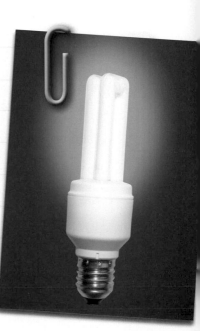

Complicated words and long sentences do not always equal good writing. The writers below have indulged themselves in writing to impress and the results are confusing for the reader. Sometimes responses are let-down by words that do not carry any sustainable meaning because they are either too simple **or** too complex.

A Average people can induce a change in the future of the environment, if they were handed certain opportunities and privileges to carry them forward towards the implementation of their lives.

B As part of the human body essentials, it is advisable that your body undergoes exercise because when this happens blood flows quicker and this enables the brain to function well, scientists say. We live in a world where science is the criterion of the things around us.

C Imperatively it would be right that nations break-off diplomatic relations with governments that have poor records in human rights because adopting such governments as allies would cause other nations like the United States to think wrong and otherwise of nations that have imbarked on diplomatic relations with government of such doings.

Re-write texts above in clear language, making whatever changes you feel are necessary so that they communicate well with the reader.

Spoken English – How far can you go in writing?

The examination you are preparing for is a test of writing skills, or to put it another way a test of 'using written language'. There is, however, a connection between spoken English and written English in the broad area of informal expression. There is also an overlap of spoken English and writing in the construction of speeches, which are sometimes entirely scripted.

The following tasks draw you into the issues of representing spoken English in writing:
- **Write a lively magazine review of fashion trends in some aspect of modern culture.**
- **Write your contribution to a national radio phone-in debate on the question 'Why are girls more violent these days?'**
- **Write a lively magazine article entitled 'How to cope with teenagers'.**

The first sample response, on fashion, takes a few risks with language. Critically, it is absolutely under control throughout the paragraph, so the informalities are part of the liveliness requested by the wording of the task. Informal English, displaying aspects of spoken English... with **style!**

It's difficult these days to keep up with trends and fashions. Even keeping up with your friends is hard enough! What's 'hot' and 'what's not' changes as often as David Beckham's hair! Not to mention the money issues. We've all been there. Your mates have decided to go 'punk' this month and you've just gone out and bought your new gear. You're chuffed with the fishnet tights, and still getting over having your nose pierced, when, quicker than you can say 'I'm a punk chick', the trend has changed and you are sooo five minutes ago!

The three short contributions to the phone-in are not as water-tight in their expression as the response above, but they are very much on-task, sensible and coherent. They include some clearly recognizable features of spoken English, as expected in responses to this task.

. . .Hi I'm John, and upon hearing the last caller I had to say my views. The last caller stated that girls aren't more violent, but I beg to differ. The reason girls are more violent is simply the mentality that is instilled in them nowadays that they have to be tough to survive. . .

. . .Hi I'm Abbie. I'm calling to put my point across. I heard the last call from a male, and I just want to make it clear, not all women are abusive, and I think it's time men stopped trying to put the blame on women when it comes to violence. If girls are more violent, then it's down to all the violent films and the pressure teenage girls are under.

. . .Hi I'm Rachael. I do believe that girls are more violent and there are influences on them. More films have girls being violent and there are a lot of violent programmes on the TV, although some girls can be as sweet as sugar and not be violent at all. The girls have gotten more violent over the last 10 years or so but there is no answer why this may be the case. Girls are sometimes treated bad by men and this could be why they are more violent.
. . .teenagers can get alcohol and drugs so easily now, and is it really only girls becoming more violent.

The following two extracts from articles on teenagers are again really promising responses; bright and engaging in both cases. Both writers appear to be very much in control of the chatty style of expression, without irritating the older reader too much!

Well. . .if you're one of the millions of parents who are asking that question then look no further, your answers are all here. We've all been there. Those god-forsaken, so-called 'golden' years between the ages of twelve and twenty. It was allegedly the 'time of our lives', but, let's face it, it wasn't. In fact, I'd even go as far as to say that my own teenage years were some of the worst of my life. The constant worrying, the 'does this top make me look fat' conversation, to which the answer always seemed to be 'yes', even when it didn't. Should I wear my hair up or down? Jeans or a skirt? Salad or pizza? It was all so completely stressful, and also completely unneeded.

Have you got door-banging, moodswinging, not-pleased-with-anything, teens? It's hard to prepare yourself when your sweet little girl, all angel faced and rosy or your hugging, smiling little boy turns into a teenager and doesn't want to hear you anymore, and instead decides to drown your voice with his own screaming voice. They don't want to listen to you when you're only trying to help and then you find yourself in fiery arguments over nothing and so stressed you could pull your own hair out, chunk by chunk.

Write your own response to one of the three exam tasks on page 169.

EXAMINER'S TIP

- Your competence in Standard English is being examined, however informal the task you may be asked to complete.
- You can use slang, but, if you are wise, you will only use it in small amounts.
- You can use features of spoken English, such as 'well' and 'you know', but don't use them too often.
- Phone-in contributions and speeches still require punctuation - in fact, it's a key way of structuring spoken language in print.
- Do not overuse slang, even if young people are your audience.

Exam Practice

> Write an article for your local newspaper about an interesting travel destination.

Sample answer

Here is an answer written by one student followed by a comment from an examiner.

Student response

A Rough guide to istanbul

The magnificant city of Istanbul is a brilliant place for tourists with it's interesting Ottoman history; it's brilliant architecture; large variety of unique and flavousome dishes and cheap shopping centres. Although this is a great city for tourists it does have it's problems for poorer people, and the traffic congestions is terrible. The growing population of the city is difficult to handle with the limited resources. There are now so many cars on the roads of Istanbul, that if you look from above you can only see long lines of coulored blocks without any road being visible. Commuting to work is a huge problem for some locals who wait for hours to reach work. This has a huge effect on economic growth, because many people spend to much time travelling instead of working. In addition to traffic there are many problems amongst the poor. Young kids try to sell flowers on the streets, just to help support their families. Many people work long hard hours in noisy crowded markets, with lots of desperate shouting over each other to gain the attention of consumers; wading their way through the huge crowds of people squashed together in the streets. Markets are particully bad in the hot summer heat, with temperatures above 40 degrees C. this heat is made worse by the body heat created by the tonnes of people crammed together, under the scolding sun. despite these discomforts of the Turkish markets, the markets supply mountainous piles of fresh varieties of exotic, juicy, colourful fruit and very low prices.

Although Istanbul has a giant stadium of three of the top footballing teams in the world, football hooligans can be a huge problem for police, which have great difficulty controling fanatic fans. A lot of crime is caused by football hooligans, including fist fights, vandalism and throwing flares. In a recent match between the two rivals of Galatasary and Fenerbache there was a terrible outbreak between the fans involved in a violent fight outside the stadium. Security guards have to take huge security measures such as shielding the players from thrown ojects, by holding up large shields like roman soldiers. Fenerbache and Galatasary fans are kept more than 15 metres away from each other by a large crowd of helmeted guards with shields. At the end of a recent match, about 200 chairs had been broken off by Galatasary fans and thrown off the top of the stadium crashing down on the floor.

Some of the architecture in Istanbul is amonst the greatest architecture in the history of the world. The huge domes covered in stylish patterns, decorations and huge towering pillars really demonstrate the brilliant talent of the ancient ottamans, before basic building material was involved. Toursits can go to these buildings and spend hours examining the ceiling in awe.

In conclusion , although there are huge problems with traffic; poor market workers; and football hooligan crime, this is one of the most magnificent cities in the world, with brilliant buildings history and cultures. It may be different for some people here but this is definitely a unique and interesting place for tourists, who want to experience somewhere different.

EXAMINER'S COMMENT

To start with a negative comment (from a jealous examiner!), there are some errors in punctuation and spelling, and marginally in sentence construction too! However....it is a magnificent response to a stimulating opportunity to write interestingly in the heat of an exam. It draws the reader in from first to last, creating an authentic sense of place. It could be seen as a high quality draft piece, requiring only very minor surgery before being publishable in a book of travel writing. Despite slips, this response would be deserving of a top grade.

How is Unit 2 assessed at GCSE?

Awareness of purpose and format: does the writing show...
- ❑ basic awareness of the purpose and format of the task?
- ❑ awareness of the purpose and format of the task?
- ❑ clear understanding of the purpose and format of the task?
- ❑ sophisticated understanding of the purpose and format of the task?

Awareness of audience: does the writing show...
- ❑ some awareness of the reader/intended audience?
- ❑ awareness of the reader/intended audience?
- ❑ clear awareness of the reader/intended audience?
- ❑ sustained awareness of the reader/intended audience?

Content and coverage: does the writing show...
- ❑ some relevant content despite uneven coverage of the topic?
- ❑ a sense of purpose shown in content coverage and some reasons are given in support of opinions and ideas?
- ❑ a clear sense of purpose shown in content coverage with appropriate reasons given in support of opinions and ideas?
- ❑ well-judged, detailed, and pertinent content coverage?

Ideas and arguments: does the writing show...
- ❑ simple sequencing of ideas providing some coherence?
- ❑ sequencing of ideas providing coherence?
- ❑ ideas shaped into coherent arguments?
- ❑ convincingly developed ideas, supported by relevant detail to construct a sophisticated argument?

Paragraphs: does the writing show...
- ❑ paragraphs used to show obvious divisions or ideas grouped into some order?
- ❑ logically ordered and sequenced paragraphs?
- ❑ paragraphs used consciously to structure the writing?
- ❑ paragraphs effectively varied in length and structure to control progression?

Style: does the writing show...
- ❑ some attempt to adapt style to purpose/audience (e.g. degree of formality)?
- ❑ a clear attempt to adapt style to purpose/audience?
- ❑ style adapted to purpose/audience?
- ❑ confident and sophisticated use of a range of stylistic devices adapted to purpose/audience?

Vocabulary: does the writing include...
- ❏ a limited range of vocabulary with little variation of word choice for meaning or effect?
- ❏ some range of vocabulary, occasionally selected to convey precise meaning or to create effect?
- ❏ a range of vocabulary selected to convey precise meaning or to create effect?
- ❏ a wide range of appropriate, ambitious vocabulary is used to create effect or convey precise meaning?

Sentence structure, punctuation and spelling: are there...
- ❏ mostly simple or compound sentences?
- ❏ compound and some complex sentences?
- ❏ grammatical structures used to vary the length and focus of sentences?
- ❏ appropriate and effective sentence structures used to achieve particular effects?

Punctuation: does the writing show...
- ❏ some attempt at punctuation where appropriate and with some accuracy?
- ❏ some control of a range of punctuation, including the punctuation of direct speech?
- ❏ a range of punctuation used accurately to structure sentences and texts?
- ❏ accurate punctuation to vary pace, clarify meaning, avoid ambiguity and create deliberate effects?

Spelling: is...
- ❏ the spelling of simple words usually accurate?
- ❏ the spelling of simple and polysyllabic words usually accurate?
- ❏ most spelling, including that of irregular words, usually accurate?
- ❏ virtually all spelling, including that of complex irregular words, correct?

Grammar – tenses and agreement: is...
- ❏ control of tense and agreement uneven?
- ❏ control of tense and agreement generally secure?
- ❏ control of tense and agreement secure?
- ❏ tense change used confidently and purposefully?

Preparing for the exam

Here are the relevant details from the GCSE specifications for this part of the assessment, including the relevant Assessment Objective for the English Language and English specifications.

GCSE ENGLISH LANGUAGE UNIT 2: Using written language

Information and ideas (20%)

Examination

You will need to complete **two** writing tasks testing transactional and discursive writing. Across the two tasks you will be asked to write for a range of audiences and purposes, adapting style to form and real-life context in, for example letters, articles, leaflets and reviews.

AO4 Writing

● Write to communicate clearly, effectively and imaginatively, using and adapting forms and selecting vocabulary appropriate to task and purpose in ways which engage the reader.

● Organize information and ideas into structured and sequenced sentences, paragraphs and whole texts, using a variety of linguistic and structural features to support cohesion and overall coherence.

● Use a range of sentence structures for clarity, purpose and effect, with accurate punctuation and spelling.

GCSE ENGLISH UNIT 2: English in the daily world (writing)

Writing: Information and ideas (20%)

Examination

You will need to complete **two** writing tasks testing transactional and discursive writing. Across the two tasks you will be asked to write for a range of audiences and purposes, adapting style to form and real-life context in, for example letters, articles, leaflets and reviews.

AO3 Writing

● Write to communicate clearly, effectively and imaginatively, using and adapting forms and selecting vocabulary appropriate to task and purpose in ways which engage the reader.

● Organize information and ideas into structured and sequenced sentences, paragraphs and whole texts, using a variety of linguistic and structural features to support cohesion and overall coherence.

● Use a range of sentence structures for clarity, purpose and effect, with accurate punctuation and spelling.

Before the day

- Practise keeping control of your work under pressure.
- Be clear about the format and organization of various types of writing.
- Look at lots of transactional writing tasks for problem-solving experience.

On the day

- Read through the tasks at the start of the exam.
- Divide your time equally between the two tasks.
- For each of the tasks in turn, take time to position yourself - take stock of the purpose and audience.
- Think through your arguments - be reasonable, but don't sit on the fence!
- Do not waste time on art and design features - it's an English exam!

Chapter 3.1 — Speaking and Listening

FOCUS ON CONTROLLED ASSESSMENT   LA UNIT 4   E UNIT 4

GCSE English Language Unit 4

GCSE English Unit 4

Students who are following the GCSE English course and those who are studying GCSE English Language work to the same requirements in Speaking and Listening.

You will be required to complete at least three Speaking and Listening tasks based on real life contexts through the exploration of ideas, texts and issues in scripted and improvised work.

The three tasks will cover the following areas:
1. communicating and adapting language
2. interacting and responding
3. creating and sustaining roles.

Taking stock of Speaking and Listening

You will have done a lot of oral work through the course of your GCSE studies, but this chapter will help you to take stock of how you can achieve your best result in the Speaking and Listening assessment.

The Speaking and Listening mark awarded to you is finally decided by your teacher's view of your overall contribution on the course, but this has to be underpinned by your work in three different areas, and in at least three different tasks. In other words, you have to earn your marks!

Speaking and Listening is at the heart of your course in English or English Language. You have to take part in a wide range of classroom tasks. You have to communicate clearly. You have to show understanding by listening and engaging.

If you don't listen, you don't learn. If you don't listen, your speaking, your writing and your understanding will suffer, because you will be out of step with the work, out of line with your teacher and out of order with your behaviour.

You will need to:

1. be prepared to give a talk – within the comfort of your own classroom
2. take a full and constructive part in all group discussions
3. be prepared to adopt a role in an everyday situation.

Take some time to think about what you are like in the classroom. Copy down the following questions and develop your answers in writing. Ask yourself honestly:

■ **Do I play a full and active part in all group discussions?**
■ **Do I always express my point of view constructively?**
■ **Do I listen with concentration to the teacher and fellow students?**
■ **Do I use Speaking and Listening skills effectively in any school activity? Which subject? Which skills?**
■ **Do I use Speaking and Listening skills effectively in any out-of-school situations? Part-time job? Hobby? Leadership role?**

EXAMINER'S TIP

Here are some sure-fire tips for success in Speaking and Listening work:

■ put your point across clearly
■ use Standard English
■ structure and organize your talk
■ adapt your style to different situations and audiences
■ listen with concentration to the teacher and fellow students
■ support and respect others
■ ask relevant questions.

Speaking and Listening tasks for every occasion

You may be asked by your teacher to do any number of the tasks from the following pages. All of them require a little thought and planning, but none of them require a huge amount of research or expert knowledge.

The best Speaking and Listening work has a clear sense of **audience** and **purpose**. So take account of **to whom** you are speaking and **why** you are speaking.

Communicating and adapting language

In all of the following examples, the focus is on the first kind of GCSE task (clear speaking in **individual contributions**). Your presentation may last up to **five minutes**, with possible extra time for you to answer questions.

Give an account of a personal experience

Even though this task is straightforward, you will need to do some planning and preparation. Using notes is allowed here, but you should avoid relying on too many of them. Reading your 'story' is not acceptable.

> **Choose one of the following:**
> - **Talk about a time when you were anxious or upset.**
> - **Talk about a time when you struggled to get something done.**
> - **Talk about an experience that frightened you.**
> - **Talk about a time when you had to convince someone to help you.**

The sense of purpose in any of the above will come from reflecting upon the lessons learned from the experience and the advice you might give others.

Present an argument for or against a local issue

In this kind of task, you should think of a local issue under dispute and take up a point of view in an informal speech, trying to persuade people to agree with you. You are more likely to make a convincing argument if you take into account opposing points of view and try to respond to them.

> - **Talk about a local facility that divides the community that is due to open or due to close.**
> - **Talk about a facility that is needed or that could be improved to better the quality of life of some people in your community.**
> - **Talk about road safety in your area, including problems and solutions.**

Lead a challenging discussion, adapting language accordingly

In this task, planning and preparation are of the utmost importance. You will be giving an opinion but this must be backed up by good, factual reasons that reflect your knowledge and understanding.

> **Choose one of the following:**
> - **In this computer age, books will soon be a thing of the past. What is your opinion?**
> - **In all aspects of life, 'good guys don't win'. Discuss.**
> - **Would the world benefit if politicians and leaders were younger?**

LITERATURE QUESTION TIME

Three or four students take their places on a 'Question Time' panel to answer possible exam questions orally on their GCSE English Literature set texts, with the rest of the class acting as the audience. The panel should have some notice of the questions, but not too much. Each member of the panel 'leads' on one question, giving as full an answer as possible. This is followed by other members of the panel offering their own comments to support or amend the argument. Questions on the author should be included where possible to stretch the quality of the responses.

Examples:
- **What does John Steinbeck say about loneliness in *Of Mice and Men*?**
- **How does Steinbeck present the character of Slim? What is the importance of Slim in the novel?**

Members of the audience should be encouraged to think of supplementary questions on themes or characters to extend the discussion.

How are individual presentations assessed?

Communicating: did you...

☐ briefly express your points of view, ideas and feelings?

☐ give straightforward but extended ideas and accounts?

☐ raise issues and points of view effectively?

☐ interpret information, ideas, feelings and points of view confidently?

☐ highlight and prioritize the essential detail of a demanding subject matter?

Adapting: did you...

☐ sometimes develop detail to add interest?

☐ begin to adapt talk and non-verbal features for different audiences?

☐ adapt talk to a variety of situations and audiences with non-verbal features added?

☐ adapt and shape talk and non-verbal features to meet different demands?

☐ use a sophisticated repertoire of strategies to meet challenging situations?

Standard English: did you...

☐ use straightforward vocabulary and grammar, with some features of Standard English?

☐ use a variety of vocabulary and structures with some reasonably accurate Standard English?

☐ use a range of well-judged sentence structures for different purposes in competent Standard English?

☐ make appropriate, controlled, effective use of Standard English vocabulary and grammar?

☐ show an assured choice and flexible use of Standard English vocabulary and grammar?

Interacting and responding

In the following tasks the priority is for you to work as part of **a team** (a pair or a small group) co-operatively (the second type of Speaking and Listening task). Remember that listening skills are just as important as speaking skills. The objective of the tasks is to come to some kind of agreement through reasoned discussion.

Discussion of a familiar topic (for example, the need for school uniform)

With these questions, you may have your own fairly fixed point of view, but try to develop your views sensibly and seriously as you listen to others.

Choose one of the following:
- **What impact do you think reality TV shows are having on our society and do you think they are a good or bad thing?**
- **What difference would winning the lottery have on you and your family?**
- **What impact would not having a computer have on your everyday life?**
- **Are girls and women more violent these days?**

Discussion of a less familiar topic (for example, a current news item or local issue)

These topics affect all of us. Try to back up your opinions with thoughtful and even topical viewpoints.

Choose one of the following:

■ **Holidays abroad are an unnecessary luxury. People should support the British economy by taking their holidays in this country. Discuss this idea and the best places to visit.**

■ **Is it worth worrying about what you eat? Develop your views.**

■ **Epidemics like swine flu are just media scare stories.**

■ **'The main purpose of school education should be to prepare young people for the workplace.' To what extent do you agree or disagree?**

Discussion arising from reading of a literary set text, or an 'unseen' poem

This task would be a personal response to the study of literature.

COLLABORATIVE TASK ON UNSEEN POETRY

Work in pairs to discuss unseen poems from past GCSE English Literature papers. In the heat of the exam an individual will be on his or her own, trying to write down sensible things in decent sentences, so this task is good practice in 'thinking skills'. Here, you will have a friend to bounce ideas around with.

■ **What is the 'voice' or the point of view that is expressed in the poem? What is the situation at the start of the poem?**

■ **Switch your attention to the ending of the poem and discuss the last comment or sentence offered by the poet. What might the poet be trying to say?**

Try both discussion exercises with several poems of different styles and structures, and discuss your conclusions with other pairs. This oral task will also help you to gain confidence in writing about poetry.

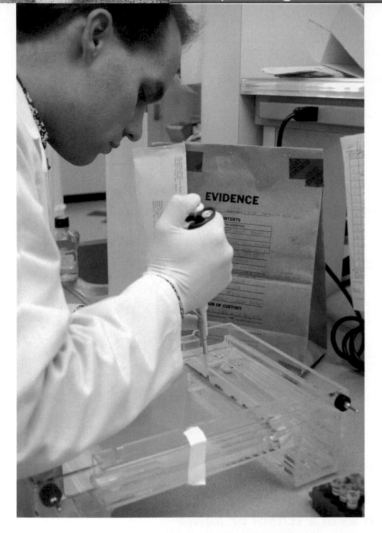

Sustained discussion of a more complex topic (for example, environmental concerns)

These questions require a little bit of national and international awareness, and they encourage you to look to the future as well.

Choose one of the following:

- **'It is the best of times, it is the worst of times.' How do you feel about life in the early 21st century?**
- **How should schools encourage more of their pupils to be interested in a career in science?**
- **What does the UK gain by having close links with Europe? Should we be doing more in terms of things such as language learning and establishing a common currency?**
- **Can ordinary people make a difference in terms of the future of the environment?**

EXAMINER'S TIP

- Remember to listen carefully and sympathetically in a discussion. When it's your turn to speak, use what you have heard to give specific responses to what others have said.

How are group discussions assessed?

Interacting: did you...
- ☐ follow the central ideas and raise straightforward questions?
- ☐ allow others to express ideas or different points of view and respond appropriately?
- ☐ engage with others' ideas and feelings, recognizing obvious bias or prejudice and referring to precise detail?
- ☐ identify useful outcomes and help structure discussion through purposeful contributions?
- ☐ initiate, develop and sustain discussion through encouraging participation and interaction, resolving differences and achieving positive outcomes?

Responding: did you...

- ☐ respond to what you heard, showing some interest, including non-verbal reactions?
- ☐ respond positively to what you heard, making helpful requests for explanation and further detail?
- ☐ listen closely and attentively, engaging with what you heard?
- ☐ challenge, develop and respond to what you heard in thoughtful and considerate ways?
- ☐ sustain concentrated listening, showing understanding of complex ideas?

Contributions: did you...

- ☐ make brief, occasional contributions and general statements in discussion?
- ☐ make specific, relevant contributions to discussion?
- ☐ make significant contributions that moved discussions forward?
- ☐ analyse and reflect on others' ideas to clarify issues and assumptions and develop the discussion?
- ☐ shape direction and content of talk, responding with flexibility to develop ideas and challenge assumptions?

Creating and sustaining roles

You will be required to act out a role in this third kind of Speaking and Listening task. You will be allowed to improvise and adapt your role on the day but preparation will increase your confidence.

Create a role in a familiar situation such as in a school or home environment

These are all situations that young people may be faced with in their own home.

Choose one of the following:

- ■ **You need to complain to your next door neighbour about their dog coming into your garden and fouling the lawn. Previously they have kept the dog tied up on a short lead. How will you deal with the problem?**
- ■ **You are a self-taught guitarist who has gradually become proficient through regular practice. Your neighbour is complaining about the noise. How are you going to resolve the situation?**
- ■ **You need to ask your parents for money for a school trip to Moscow. You have just had to ask for money for music lessons. How are you going to get the money from them?**

Develop and sustain a role in a less familiar situation such as in a shop or office environment

These are all community-based situations. Ensure you use appropriate language, punctuation and tone in this task. Plan the conversation to ensure you get a positive outcome.

Choose one of the following:

- **You are a local shopkeeper who regularly serves schoolchildren. You have to ask a student for ID in order to purchase a DVD. The student is unhappy about this as he is with a group of friends. How do you go about this as you do not wish to lose customers?**

- **You are an office supervisor who has to deal with the theft of office supplies within your team of three people. You need to find the culprit and deal with them.**

- **A customer queries their change, claiming that the cashier gave them the change for £5 rather than £10. You are the supervisor who arrives at the checkout to deal with the irate customer and an upset cashier.**

Create a complex character in a challenging role in an unfamiliar environment such as a council meeting or planning enquiry

Your tone, use of language and focus on strategic points of reference will ensure success. In these situations you must be on top of your game.

Choose one of the following:

- **You are a governor at school who strongly feels that future funding needs to be spent on sports facilities rather than on IT equipment. You are being given the opportunity to speak at a meeting with the Head Teacher and other governors. You have 15 minutes to convince them to allocate the money to sports.**

- **You are a local councillor talking to local residents about plans to build a large supermarket just out of town, threatening the future prosperity of the traditional town-centre shops.**

- **You are an architect who wants to build 50 new eco-friendly houses on a field behind an existing housing estate in a village. You will need to present this idea to the local council.**

Create an improvisation as a pair or group based on one of the texts studied

You could link this task to one of your GCSE set texts.

The simplest and often most effective way of taking a role in a literature context is using dramatic monologue, where your challenge is to empathize with a character from a play or novel.

Choose one of the following:

- Choose a character from one of your set texts. Imagine you are that character at the end of the 'story'. Speak the character's thoughts as he or she reflects privately on the events that have occurred.

- With a partner improvise a dialogue between two characters from one of your set texts. The dialogue should look back on events that have occurred.

These responses should not be scripted, but a short planning session is in order to think through the content of the improvisation and to develop a sense of the personality of your chosen character.

Remember that the role-play needs to offer something different from the pages of the text. In other words, it should not be a near-repeat of a scene from the book.

How is role-play assessed?

Creating: did you...
- ❑ draw upon ideas to create a simple character?
- ❑ create a straightforward character using speech, gesture and movement?
- ❑ sustain a role through appropriate use of language and effective gestures and movement?
- ❑ create a convincing character role using a range of techniques?
- ❑ create a complex, challenging character with a choice of dramatic approaches?

Sustaining: did you...
- ❑ react to situations showing some understanding of relationships and familiar ideas?
- ❑ engage with situations, showing understanding of issues and relationships?
- ❑ help to develop situations and ideas, showing understanding and insight into relationships and significant issues?
- ❑ respond skillfully and sensitively to explore ideas, issues and relationships?
- ❑ explore and respond to complex ideas, issues and relationships?

EXAMINER'S TIP

- ■ Remember when working in role, try to get into character and remain in character throughout. If you fall back into your own personality, you will lose marks.

Using English in the daily world

Speaking and Listening skills in the world of work

Here are two accounts by people in very different jobs, of the ways in which they use their Speaking and Listening skills at work. Read each account carefully before completing the tasks.

A

The sales manager

Having worked in a sales role for over 15 years in various industries, I find there are some key skills that are essential if you are to be successful in this chosen profession.

Having attended many sales training courses, the key thing I learnt was that the total impact of a message is about 10% verbal (words only) and 40% vocal (including tone of voice, inflection and other sounds) and 50% non-verbal. The non-verbal can include how you respond to your audience; listening to them and answering effectively is key.

Every day in sales you meet different people, some more open to your product than others, but none of them would have agreed to that meeting if they did not have a need. So the greetings are always friendly, but then I ask open questions that are relevant. I listen to them and gather all the information I need in order to sell the right product to them.

The key to a good sale is ensuring I have heard what the customer says and then recapping it back to them, which shows I have listened and understood. Then I present my products based on this need. It's called 'selling features and benefits', followed by closed questions (questions with yes or no answers), to get to the sale.

Speaking and Listening skills are essential to my success. Effective communication also makes the customer feel that they have had a good experience rather than a 'hard sell', which no one enjoys and which would never result in future business.

Police officer

As a working police officer in the local community, my speaking and listening skills are vital to every part of my job. I meet the same people every week as I walk around the village and stop to talk to the local shopkeepers to find out what is going on and what I need to know. This means I need to be asking the right questions in order to gain the information, but more importantly, listening to the answers I am given. If I didn't listen, I wouldn't find out, and I think I would also start to annoy the locals, as I would probably have to ask again later in the week!

> "If I couldn't communicate and listen, I would not make a good local police officer."

I speak to everyone: children, teenagers, pensioners. They all have something different to say. Some may be happy with the community; others want to see some change. I do my best to give truthful, appropriate answers but some things I cannot change and I don't think they expect me to be able to. It just allows the individual to get it off their chest.

Communicating and adapting language

Your own English skills (oral, reading and writing) may be particularly challenged on a work experience placement. If you have been on one of these placements, write a summary of how you used these skills. If you have not yet been on a work experience placement, imagine which skills you might use in this situation.

Interacting and responding

In a group, discuss the qualities required by each of the two people in the examples above in order to carry out their jobs effectively. Which qualities are the same? Which ones are different? Remember to listen to other students' opinions and respond to them appropriately when you speak.

Creating and sustaining roles

Choose a profession that requires good Speaking and Listening skills. Make notes about how the skills might be used, then role-play the person talking about the necessary Speaking and Listening skills for his or her particular job.

Employer/employee meeting: Two versions

In this imaginary situation, an employee has been called into a meeting with a manager to discuss unsatisfactory timekeeping and to receive a verbal warning for his or her behaviour. Two versions of the same situation are given below.

VERSION A

Manager: Thank you for coming to the meeting. I would like to discuss the fact that you have been consistently late for work and have been taking a lot of sick days over the last couple of months. Before we discuss this situation in full and what I am going to do about it, I would like to give you the opportunity to explain why this has been happening.

Employee: I know I have been late and have been off sick, but I am struggling at home at the moment.

Manager: Do you want to talk about it, as it's affecting your performance at work and we therefore need to do something about it?

Employee: I have a child minder who is not well at the moment and I can't find anyone else to help me out on those days, so I thought it was easier to call in sick, rather than lose all my holiday.

Manager: But did you not consider discussing this with me, rather than having your attendance and sick record looked at?

Employee: No, as you never know if it would be frowned on that I can't sort out my childcare arrangements, and I need to work, and I love my job.

Manager: Well, that is all good to hear. What we need to do is try to sort it out before it becomes a real issue. You need to look for other methods of childcare that will be more reliable and allow you to get in on time and regularly. Maybe we can ask other people in the office who they use and that may help. What do you think?

Employee: That would be great, thank you. I do want to get it sorted as I am worried.

Manager: Well, let's do that first and see whether it can be sorted out. In the meantime, I need your assurance that you will not phone in sick at those times and will be in on time in future. We can monitor the situation and review it in a month's time. Does that seem fair to you?

Employee: Yes, thank you. I will do my best.

VERSION B

Manager: Thanks for coming to this meeting. I want to let you know that I am unhappy with your constant lateness for work and the number of days you have called in sick recently. What's happening?

Employee: I know I have been late a couple of times and have been off sick, but I am struggling at home at the moment.

Manager: Right. But you need to get here on time and be in the office, otherwise everyone suffers because we are short-staffed.

Employee: I do understand that but...

Manager: Good. Well, if you understand that, it must stop and I need to give you a verbal warning for your file. Do you understand that?

Employee: Yes, but I would like to try to sort it out first.

Manager: Well, it should have been sorted out before it came to this. What seems to be the problem?

Employee: I keep being let down by my child minder and this is causing me problems.

Manager: So, what you are saying is that you do not have childcare sufficient to allow you to do your job properly?

Employee: No, I love my job and am trying to sort it out.

Manager: Well, I suggest you take a couple of days of annual leave, sort it out and come back to me to tell me this won't happen again. We can then monitor it and review in a month's time. Off you go now.

Communicating and adapting language

Give a presentation on what makes a good leader. Talk about the skills required to successfully hold a position of responsibility, especially as a young person. Make sure you give examples where someone has not shown good leadership and also examples where someone has shown good leadership skills when dealing with a tricky situation. What makes a good teacher, captain, manager?

Interacting and responding

There is no indication in the two versions of the script whether the manager and employee is male or female. In a group, discuss in detail by referring to the text, the behaviour of both, and consider if the gender of the participants would make any difference to the outcome.

Creating and sustaining roles

Imagine that you are the new manager of a hotel. Give a pep talk to your staff, outlining a set of principles to work to. The hotel has done well previously but you want it to continue to improve. You want to suggest gently to the staff that there may be changes, but you do not want to rattle them.

Real world role-plays

Role-play 1: Dealing with a customer complaint

In this task, one person will play the role of a clothes shop employee who is receiving a complaint and a second person will play the role of the customer who is making a complaint. The class will observe the role-play and make notes about what they see and hear.

Customer: You have bought a shirt and it has shrunk after being washed once. You bought the shirt last week, but it is now reduced by £15 as a sale item.

Employee: You are working behind the till and your manager is out at the bank. The customer is complaining that the shirt has shrunk but you have noticed that it also has a small tear. The shop has a policy that no refunds are to be given if there is evidence to suggest that the item has been worn.

The class: Evaluate how effectively each role was played. Consider the following:
● How did each student answer questions? Did he or she fully understand the questions asked or ask for clarification where necessary?
● Did the student playing the employee listen and react appropriately to the complaint? Did he or she ask questions to be fully satisfied before making any decision on the course of action?
● What was the employee's objective? Was it to make sure the customer was happy or to uphold the shop's policy in the manager's absence?

Role-play 2: Applying for funding

In this task, one person will play the role of a student representative applying for money from the Head Teacher and senior management. The class (or a group of students) will play the roles of this senior management team.

Student representative: You are asking for funding on behalf of a number of students who would like to study a specific course and need extra equipment in order to do so. The course could be media based (for example, radio equipment), hairdressing (beauty equipment), or something similar. The school has money available, but it needs to fund a number of courses. You need to convince the Head Teacher that your course is valuable to the school and the local area.

Questions to consider before the discussion:
- How much are you asking for?
- What are you prepared to accept?
- How will providing this money benefit the school?
- What research could you do to make your argument more convincing?

The class: Evaluate the effectiveness of the presentation. Consider the following:
- Has the speaker prepared well? Has he or she done enough research on the course and its needs, as well as its benefit to the school and its students?
- Did he or she listen to feedback and respond appropriately?
- Did the speaker ask enough questions to gain the right information about the budget?
- did the speaker achieve his or her objectives by the end of the presentation or at least gain some agreement on the next steps?

Role-play 3: Asking for a pay rise

In this task, one person will play the role of an employee at an office, garage or shop who is asking for a pay rise, and a second person will play the employee's manager.

Employee: You have been working for the company for two years and have always had good reviews and positive feedback from management and customers. You now feel that you deserve a pay rise and have arranged a meeting with your manager. Other members of staff with the same level or experience are being paid an extra £500 a year.

Questions to consider before the discussion:
- Do you have your review information or letters from customers to refer to?
- How much are you asking to receive and what would you accept?
- Have you looked into what others are being paid?

Manager: The company is not doing very well at the moment so money is tight. However, you have a lot of respect for the employee and value their contribution.

The class: Evaluate how effectively each role was played. Consider the following:
- Has the employee prepared for the meeting?
- Did the employee open the conversation stating what he or she wanted?
- Have both the employee and the manager listened to the answers given and responded appropriately?
- Are both the manager and employee happy with the final result and have they achieved the objective they set out to achieve?

Preparing for the Speaking and Listening Assessment

Here are the relevant details from the GCSE specifications for this part of the assessment, including the Assessment Objective relevant to both specifications (these are the skills you are trying to show to gain marks and grades):

GCSE ENGLISH LANGUAGE UNIT 4: Spoken Language

Using language (20%)

Assessment

Candidates will be required to complete at least three Speaking and Listening tasks based on real life contexts through the exploration of ideas, texts and issues in scripted and improvised work. The three tasks will cover the following areas:
- communicating and adapting language
- interacting and responding
- creating and sustaining roles.

AO1 Speaking and Listening

- Speak to communicate clearly and purposefully; structure and sustain talk, adapting it to different situations and audiences; use Standard English and a variety of techniques as appropriate.
- Listen and respond to speakers' ideas, perspectives and how they construct and express their meanings.
- Interact with others, shaping meanings through suggestions, comments and questions and drawing ideas together.
- Create and sustain different roles.

GCSE ENGLISH UNIT 4:

Speaking and Listening (20%)

Assessment

Candidates will be required to complete at least three Speaking and Listening tasks based on real life contexts through the exploration of ideas, texts and issues in scripted and improvised work. The three tasks will cover the following areas:

- communicating and adapting language
- interacting and responding
- creating and sustaining roles.

AO1 Speaking and Listening

- Speak to communicate clearly and purposefully; structure and sustain talk, adapting it to different situations and audiences; use Standard English and a variety of techniques as appropriate.
- Listen and respond to speakers' ideas, perspectives and how they construct and express their meanings.
- Interact with others, shaping meanings through suggestions, comments and questions and drawing ideas together.
- Create and sustain different roles.

EXAMINER'S TIP

- The table below shows the key areas to bear in mind when taking part in Speaking and Listening work.

Participation	Communication	Understanding
• Take a full and active part in all group discussions. • Be prepared to give a talk to the class. • Be prepared to adopt a role in a drama-focused activity.	• Put your point across clearly. • Use Standard English. • Structure and organize your talk. • Adapt your style to different situations.	• Listen with concentration to the teacher and fellow students. • Support and respect others. • Ask relevant questions.

How to be a good speaker

- Do not stray from the topic being discussed.
- Do not repeat points that have already been made, unless you have something new to add.
- Establish eye contact with your audience; do not stare at the floor or out of the window.
- If you are making a short contribution, rehearse it in your mind before saying it aloud. Also, your first sentence of a longer contribution should be clear.
- Always try to make at least one relevant contribution in a discussion.
- If you are nervous try to get a comment in early.
- Do not interrupt other speakers. In discussion, it is a matter of judgement when to intervene. Wait patiently for an opening before making your comment.
- Always be polite.
- Vary the tone of your voice; do not speak in a monotone.
- Do not monopolize a discussion; allow others to speak.
- Be enthusiastic (or at least positive) about the topic or task.
- When you talk to an audience, make sure that your body language is positive; do not lean or slouch.
- Do not place your hand over your mouth when speaking.

How to be a good listener

- Always be involved in discussions, even if you are just listening carefully to what is being said.
- Do not yawn or look bored.
- When listening to a speaker, face them and give them your full attention. Consider your body language; you should look as if you are listening. For instance, leaning forward attentively.
- Encourage other, nervous speakers by means of the occasional nod and smile.

Tips for interacting with you audience

- When giving a talk vary your methods of communication – for example consider using visual aides or building multimedia elements into your presentation.
- If the topic of your talk allows it, consider including a practical demonstration (for example: applying make-up to a model; coaching a particular skill).
- Consider changing the location of your talk or using a seating plan (for example: a computer room, gym, lecture hall).
- Using rhetorical questions can make your listeners think, but if you really want to keep the members of your audience on their toes, you could consider asking one or two of them a direct question.
- If you choose to use 'direct questioning', use it sparingly to help illustrate a point. Keep your questions short and simple and ensure you are fairly confident about what the other person will say. For example: 'How many people do you think fail their driving test each year? I can tell you that the answer actually is…'
- Encourage your audience to ask questions at the end of your presentation. Think about the kind of questions that are likely to come up in advance, so that you can offer considered and informative responses.

FOCUS ON CONTROLLED ASSESSMENT

LA UNIT 4

GCSE English Language Unit 4

You will be required to study and complete an assignment on an aspect of spoken language. The assignment will be a sustained response to your own or others' uses of spoken language. In other words, you have to write an essay in answer to a question about talk.

The spoken language study is worth 10% of your total marks.

In this chapter, you will become familiar with the areas of study broadly involved in the study of spoken language, which will be new to you at GCSE. You will move towards the Controlled Assessment task that will be set by your teacher(s), following the general instructions issued by the WJEC.

Before you complete your Controlled Assessment, you will have to research a topic. You may need to listen to recordings, study transcripts, and recall from memory how people have used spoken language in situations that you have experienced.

Recordings: These could be audio only, or audio-visual. What do you think are the advantages of using recordings for a spoken language study? What are the disadvantages?

Transcripts: A transcript is a written version of a recording of spoken language. It attempts to represent accurately the features of spoken English that are different from standard written English. What do you think are the advantages of having a transcript of speech available? What are the difficulties of creating a transcript?

Recollections: Recollections are memories; in this case, memories of the way spoken language has been used interestingly in your experience, in relation to a topic you are researching. How can you use recollections of speech? What are the shortcomings (or problems) of recollections?

Differences between writing and speech

There are many important differences between spoken and written language, apart from the fact, that one is heard and one is read. For example, when using written language, you write in sentences and use full-stops, commas, question marks and exclamation marks as punctuation. When using spoken language, you are able to use intonation, volume and pauses instead.

> **Make a list of the differences between spoken English and written English.**

Features of spoken English

Spoken English is sometimes rambling and sometimes stuttering. Speech needs to be coherent and meaningful, and as far as possible, grammatical. However, there are always likely to be some lapses in fluency:

> "Well, I'm... I'm not sure I can help you, I could help if I ...er... had a bit more ready cash... and... you should've given me some notice really shouldn't you? I mean, I mean I would've liked to have helped but..."

Here are some features of spoken English:
- unpolished or run-on sentences
- hesitations, pauses
- repetitions
- fillers (a word or sound filling a pause)
- contractions (shortened forms)
- colloquial or loose vocabulary
- tag questions (i.e. at the end of the sentence).

> **Look at the sample of speech on page 201 and find examples of each of the listed features of spoken English.**

Spoken language study

Reading transcripts

As a GCSE student, you are not required to create a transcript, but you may be required to read one as part of your study of spoken language.

- The transcript of a prepared speech will show polished, fluent prose, with none of the blips that characterize spontaneous speech.

- At GCSE, you can quote short items of spoken English with references to pauses (...), fillers (er, um) and words which have been underlined for emphasis. Features of punctuation, especially stops, questions, and exclamations, are also important. Unfinished sentences will be accurately represented in transcripts.

Here are two examples of transcripts of pupils talking in a classroom environment. The first example is a short extract to whet your appetite for a discussion on hoodies worn by teenagers.

Lloyd	...and I think you can see the amount of people wearing hoodies, people think just because lots of people wear them, they're bad.
Ahmed	Could just be another trend, it could end.
Rachel	I don't think it's right to ban hoodies altogether, because psychologists have started to warn parents and teachers that you need to be able to express yourself and wearing a hoodie is part of that, so...

The second extract is from a role-play involving a local resident and a teenager who has been given an ASBO.

Alex	If a policeman says you've done a crime, I'll think you'll find that you've probably done it.
Lloyd	Nah, I ain't done nothing.
Alex	Then why were you being tried fairly in a court and were being found guilty then?
Lloyd	Cos it's just stereotyping bro!
Alex	Stereotyping?

Think of a brief comment of two or three sentences to make about each of the short extracts above and on the previous page.

Writing about spoken language

Although a spoken language study is something that you may not have done before, you will soon gain confidence to make relevant and effective observations. Here are a few isolated sentences from students' essays just to show the kinds of things that could be said about spoken English:

There are various examples which show us that this is spontaneous speech, for example, the recurring regular pauses in the middle of sentences...

False starts and self-corrections also demonstrate speech, but also convey the nerves of the speaker.

There is an example of informal speech, "well hang on a minute", which changes the tone and formality of the text.

The use of interruptions also emphasizes that the texts are genuine spoken language.

- What do you think 'spontaneous speech' is?
- What might 'false starts and self-corrections' be in spoken language?
- What is 'informal speech'?
- What are 'interruptions'?

How spoken language is used in different contexts

In order to gain a wider understanding of spoken language you need to consider a number of different contexts, and understand the features of both private and public speech; for example, a conversation between yourself and a friend and a speech made by a politician.

In the workplace

Your own experience of 'the world of work' may be confined to work experience and part-time employment. You may, however, have some understanding of pressures in the workplace.

For example, the following comment might be made by one employee to another:

> When Alison took over as boss, she said that she wouldn't make the same mistakes as Phil did, but she is, of course. He would put notices up on the wall rather than speak to us, and that's what she's doing. She even put a new notice on top of one of his old ones. When I pointed it out, she said it was quicker. She's insecure, but she won't admit it.

Questions for discussion:
- **How do work colleagues speak and behave towards each other?**
- **How do employers and supervisors speak and behave to their employees and the people they manage?**

Use evidence from recordings, transcripts and recollections to answer these questions.

On television

Your experience of television will include live programmes for children and young adults. No doubt it also includes live sports programmes and blockbuster reality programmes like *Strictly Come Dancing* and *The X Factor*.

For example:

> I enjoy listening to the panel arguing more than watching the dancing. It's all stage-managed though. It's spontaneous, but very well-rehearsed, or at least set up.

Questions for discussion:

■ **Consider one of your favourite programmes. How is spoken language used in the programme to make it interesting to the viewer?**

Watch an episode of your chosen programme and take notes. Refer to your notes as evidence when answering the question above.

In the classroom

This is your home ground. Teaching and learning methods are changing rapidly. It is not just new technology that has made a difference to the way young people learn; it is the classroom management skills that the best teachers now use.

Questions can be used to bring the class to order, to make polite requests, to rebuke, to set the topic, to elicit information, to create a co-operative mood and to give commands. Interactions typically include questioning by both teachers and pupils.

For example:

> Baz taught my dad, and it sounds as if he hasn't changed at all over the years. We always have a laugh in his lessons, but we know who's the boss.

Questions for discussion:

■ **How do students work together to learn effectively in the classroom?**

■ **How might a teacher skillfully use questioning skills in the classroom?**

Record and/or transcribe a classroom interaction or by close observation and note-making, show the importance of questioning skills in the classroom.

Problem solving

Giving directions that are clear and reliable is important on occasion. It ought to be straightforward, but so often is not. Explaining a procedure to someone can sometimes be very complicated, and you can make a complete mess of it. Making decisions can be problematic too, especially where two or more people have to agree. These are all everyday problems that have to be solved using spoken language.

Think of an example of someone providing directions. They could be directions for how to get somewhere or how to do something. Use notes, personal experience and recollections to provide evidence. How do you think people could become more skilful at everyday problem-solving, such as giving directions, explaining procedures and making decisions?

How spoken language is adapted to different listeners

In everyday life you adapt your spoken language to meet the expectations of other people. The way you speak could differ depending on factors such as the age of your listener, his or her authority or the formality of the conversation.

Responding to older or younger listeners

You can perhaps surprise yourself with the level of skill you have when adapting your language to talk to older and younger people. However, you still need to think about what you say and how you say it, in order to develop a dialogue with someone who is not in your immediate circle of friends. For example, you may need to take the listener's level of knowledge about the subject into account, or simplify your language when speaking to very young children.

For example:

> I've decided to take a bit of extra care when I speak to people much older or much younger than me – how come some of them know much more about computers than I do, for instance?

Questions for discussion:
- **How do people speak and behave when talking and responding to primary school and pre-school children?**
- **How do people speak and behave when talking and responding to elderly people?**

Use evidence from recorded conversations and/or close observation and note-taking.

Responding to people in authority

The status and power of speakers may affect how they speak and behave. This balance of power may be affected by factors such as age, occupation, gender, and context.

For example:

> It's probably best to start by assuming people in positions of authority deserve to be respected when you speak to them. Most of the time it's true, though sometimes you need to stand firm.

Questions for discussion:
- **How do young people speak and behave when talking and responding to people in authority, such as a Head Teacher?**

Try to consider evidence from school life, work experience and life in the community in your answer.

Talking to friends and family

Between friends or family members most talk is informal and spontaneous because it takes place between people who know one another. However, even between friends and family, the formality of a conversation can differ. For example, a parent may modify what they say to their spouse when their children are around.

For example:

> I know how much I can get away with, but I try to remember not to be too cheeky when our kid is around.

Responding to 'unfamiliar adults'

Sometimes it isn't easy to predict the level of formality that a conversation requires when talking to someone unfamiliar. In these situations, you may need to remain relatively formal until you have established the tone of conversation. If, for example, the person is friendlier than you expected, you may not wish to try your luck by becoming over-familiar.

For example:

> One of the things to remember is — if the person is friendlier than you expected, don't push your luck by becoming over-familiar and chummy!

> **Question for discussion:**
> - **How do young people speak and behave when talking and responding to unfamiliar adults?**
>
> **Use evidence from transcripts and personal experience, and possibly examples from the media.**

Standard and non-standard forms of spoken language

In some situations it is important to speak as correctly as possible. In other situations you can take a more relaxed attitude. Sometimes you can go out of your way to speak in a non-standard way by using a local regional dialect, a youth dialect, or the speech of a specific group.

For example:

> My mum keeps telling me not to speak 'slang' because it lets me down, but she doesn't realize how important it is to speak street language as well.

Look at the list of examples of non-standard speech below. Add examples from your own dialect to the list.

- double negatives ("I won't do nothing")
- parts of verbs ("I seen her")
- pronouns ("Look at them boys")
- comparatives and superlatives ("Sam's more cleverer than me")
- subject-verb agreements ("There isn't no buses running")
- prepositions ("Come over by here")
- choice of vocabulary ("wee bairn")

Question for discussion:
- **How do people use non-standard spoken English positively in your community?**

Write down some specific examples.

Controlled Assessment Practice

Read the following example transcript below. The transcript records a discussion that took place between a group of students in a classroom environment, regarding the problems caused by wearing hoodies.

Lloyd: I think the minority of people that wear hoods actually go out with the intent to commit a crime or violent act, and I think it's this minority that's being shown on the news and being shown by the media and the majority of people who wear a hood just get pushed to the side and the media don't say anything about them but it's the violent crimes that happen that are shown in the media and this is what gives people wearing hoodies a bad name...

Alex: (interrupts) but what causes them...

Lloyd: and I don't understand that.

Alex: But what causes them to actually commit the crimes then? There's many possible reasons, a lot of it is caused by gangs hanging around on the streets and they have nothing else to do – so that's all they seem to be able to do, just go out and entertain themselves and all they can find to do is commit crimes.

Lloyd: I can see that you think that if someone was wearing a hoodie they might be trying to commit a crime or whatever but I think it's mainly the person inside. I can see how wearing a hoodie would lower your morale and your morals and you'd think maybe the cameras can't see you or whatever but I think it's mainly dependent on the person inside the hoodie, cos if you were to go out and you weren't a violent person or a criminal and you wore a hoodie, would you because you're wearing a hoodie think, oh I'll commit a crime.

David: You mentioned the cameras then though, you know there's obviously a problem with CCTV, people have got used to, you know, the Nanny State, Big Brother being around. Britain has 20% of the world's CCTV cameras, and what was it, more cameras in Basingstoke than in New York, which is quite bad actually but... this has obviously made people paranoid but in turn people have also became paranoid about the hoods, so it's almost a generalization, you know sort of everybody who wears hoods is bad. In Bluewater 23% more people go to Bluewater ever since they banned hoodies. But I can't personally see how anybody would actually dare to commit a crime in a major shopping centre in daylight.

Alex: I think the amount of people there has increased because of all the publicity, the media reaction to the problem, it could just be a publicity stunt.

David: The government has backed it hasn't it?

Alex: Think so... but...

David: probably a vote winner, because these youths who wear the hoodies, they can't vote against the government in next election but the people who they are supposed to be protecting can vote against the government, so the government has to be seen to be doing something.

How effective is this discussion in persuading you that teenagers who wear hoodies are unfairly treated in society?

Look at:
- what the participants say
- how they say it
- how the discussion is organized.

Sample answer

Read the example response below and comments from the examiner.

Student response

There are some interesting points raised in this discussion and I think it's clear that some of the speakers have strong beliefs about what they say. Lloyd for example, uses a lot of repetition to put his point across at the start: "I think the minority of people that wear hoods actually go out with the intent to commit a crime" and "I think it's the minority that's being shown on the news". The use of 'minority' stresses how stereotypes are created about teenagers and how this is unfair.

David's points are persuasive, because he uses actual examples to back up his points: "In Bluewater 23% more people go to Bluewater ever since they banned hoodies". This example grips the attention of the other members too, because Alex reacts to this directly in his response: "it could just be a publicity stunt". The way people react to this point shows that it is worth thinking about.

Alex does not get many chances to speak in the discussion. He gets interrupted a lot, perhaps because he hesitates at times which prompts others to jump in. This makes his points less persuasive because he doesn't seem to be as committed to them.

EXAMINER'S COMMENT

The student makes some valid observations about the speakers in this discussion and selects appropriate evidence from the transcript to back-up these points. Some of the quotations are perhaps overlong in places and these could be better integrated into the writing. The student remains focused on the question throughout and refers to how the participants speak as well as what they say. More could perhaps be said about how Lloyd has a tendency to dominate at the start of the discussion, making it difficult for Alex to speak.

How is spoken language assessed at GCSE?

Awareness of spoken language: is there...
- ❏ limited awareness of how spoken language is used?
- ❏ Some awareness of how speakers use spoken language?
- ❏ Clear awareness of how spoken language is adapted?
- ❏ Confident awareness of how spoken language is adapted?
- ❏ Confident awareness of how spoken language is selected and adapted?

Influences: is there...
- ❏ limited understanding of factors that influence spoken language?
- ❏ Some understanding of the main influences on speakers' language choices?
- ❏ Clear understanding of the different influences on speakers' language choices?
- ❏ Sound understanding of significant influences on speakers' language choices?
- ❏ Sophisticated understanding of subtle influences on speakers' language choices?

Speech variations: is there...
- ❏ some ability to explain obvious differences in language?
- ❏ Some limited ability to explain how differences in speech may affect communication?
- ❏ Understanding and explanation of the effects of speech variations?
- ❏ Clear explanation of the significance of speech variations?
- ❏ Perceptive explanation of the impact of significant features of speech variations?

Language change: is there...
- ❏ some ability to analyse and evaluate variations and changes in spoken language?
- ❏ Some limited ability to analyse and evaluate how language changes?
- ❏ Ability to analyse and evaluate how language changes?
- ❏ Clear ability to analyse and evaluate effects of language changes?
- ❏ Sustained ability to analyse and evaluate susceptibility to variation and features of language change?

Preparing for Controlled Assessment

Here are the relevant details from the GCSE specification for this part of the assessment, including the relevant Assessment Objective for the English Language specification.

GCSE ENGLISH LANGUAGE UNIT 4: Spoken Language

Studying spoken language: Variations, choices, change in spoken language (10%)

Controlled Assessment

You will need to write **one** written study of spoken language.

Ac...dgements

...nd author would like to thank the following for their ...reproduce photographs and other copyright material: T...t: Serg64/Shutterstock; **p14m:** Herbert Kratky/ ... **p14b:** Pichugin Dmitry/Shutterstock; **p15:** Graham ...rary; **p16-17:** Gail Johnson/Shutterstock; **p18t:** Sinopix/ ...; **p18b:** Rolf Hicker Photography/Photolibrary; **p19:** Mark ...ex Features; **p22:** Alex Livesey/Getty Images Sport/Getty ...**7:** Topical Press Agency/Hulton Archive/Getty Images; **p29:** ...key/Rex Features; **p37:** Image100/OUP; **p39:** Milena Lachowicz/ ...ock; **p40t:** David Berry/Shutterstock; **p40-41:** zhu difeng/ ...ock; **p41t:** Tatiana Grozetskaya/Shutterstock; **p41b:** John Riley/ ...is; **p42-43:** Andrei Rybachuk/Shutterstock; **p45:** Eric Gevaert/ ...tock; **p46:** Morten Hilmer/Shutterstock; **p47:** Andreas Gradin/ ...stock; **p48:** Sergey Kurnikov/Dreamstime; **p54-55:** Photodisc/ ...**56:** Carlos Arranz/Shutterstock; **p59:** Paul Popper/Popperfoto/ ...Images; **p61:** Rusty Elliott/Big Stock Photo; **p64:** Photodisc/OUP; ...Trinity Mirror/Mirrorpix/Alamy; **p69:** Roberto Cerruti/Shutterstock; ...Mikael Damkier/Shutterstock; **p75l:** Stringer/Getty Images; **p75m:** ...on-Hibbert/Rex Features; **p75r:** The Art Archive/Alamy; **p77:** English ...ool/The Bridgeman Art Library/Getty Images; **p80b:** Ronald Grant ...rchive; **p81t:** Donald Cooper/Photostage; **p81b:** Alastair Muir/Rex ...eatures; **p90-91:** Corbis/OUP; **p93:** MGM/The Kobal Collection/Cooper, Andrew; **p94:** Reuters/Corbis; **p95:** c.Icon/Everett/Rex Features; **p100:** Tischenko Irina/Shutterstock; **p102:** Working Title/The Kobal Collection/ Sparham: **p104:** Andrey Shadrin/Shutterstock; **p107:** Denis Vrublevski/ Shutterstock; **p108:** Douglas Mccarthy/Mary Evans Picture Library; **p109:** Castle Rock/Columbia/The Kobal Collection; **p110:** Everett Collection/ Rex Features; **p113:** Ronald Grant Archive; **p114:** Ronald Grant Archive; **p117:** Everett Collection/Rex Features; **p118:** Ronald Grant Archive; **p119:** Ronald Grant Archive; **p122:** Feng Yu/Shutterstock; **p124:** Karkas/ Shutterstock; **p125:** Fox Searchlight/The Kobal Collection; **p126:** David Fisher/Rex Features: **p133:** M_ART/Shutterstock; **p134:** Manor Photography/Alamy; **p135:** Factoria singular fotografia/Shutterstock; **p136:** Photos 12/Alamy; **p137:** mehmetcan/Shutterstock; **p138:** Paul Banton/Shutterstock; **p139:** grynold/Shutterstock; **p141:** Robert Daly/ Getty; **p142l:** Voronin76/Shutterstock; **p142r:** baki/Shutterstock; **p153:** Laurence Gough/Shutterstock; **p155t:** Photodisc/OUP; **p155b:** Mona Makela/Dreamstime; **p156t:** Clara/Shutterstock; **p156m:** Palabra/ Shutterstock; **p156b:** Tetra Images/OUP; **p158:** Tetra Images/OUP; **p159:** Mav/Dreamstime; **p160l:** Anthony Charlton/AP Photo; **p160r:** Phil Walter/ Getty Images Sport/Getty Images; **p161t:** Karel Gallas/Shutterstock; **p161m:** Eddie Keogh/Reuters; **p161b:** Ben Stansall/AFP; **p163:** Hartmut Schmidt/Photolibrary; **p164:** Ray Stubblebine/Reuters; **p167:** Zerra/ Shutterstock; **p168t:** Rex Features; **p168b:** Christoph Weihs/Shutterstock; **p169:** Helmut Meyer Zur Capellen/Photolibrary; **p173:** Senai Aksoy/ Shutterstock; **p177:** c./Shutterstock; **p178t:** Comstock/OUP; **p182b:** Monkey Business Images/Fotolia; **p180:** Adrian Sherratt/Alamy; **p183:** Rex Features; **p184:** Hinochika/Shutterstock; **p185:** Corbis/Digital Stock/ OUP; **p186:** Karen Moskowitz/Getty Images; **p187:** Valueline/OUP; **p188:** Paul Doyle/Alamy; **p190:** Photodisc/OUP; **p191:** Pawel Libera/Photolibrary; **p192:** Yuri Arcurs/Shutterstock; **p194:** AL Accardo/Masterfile; **p195:** endostock/Fotolia; **p196:** John Penezic/Shutterstock; **p198:** Masterfile; **p199t:** Photodisc/OUP; **p199b:** VladKol/Shutterstock; **p200t:** Yuri Arcurs/Shutterstock; **p200m:** Design Pics/OUP; **p200b:** Comstock/OUP; **p202:** BananaStock/OUP; **p206:** Blend Images/OUP; **p207:** Yuri Arcurs/ Shutterstock; **p209:** Jim Laws/Alamy.
Cover image: GlowImages/Alamy

Illustrations by Mark Brierley, Emmanuel Cerisier, Martin Sanders and Rory Walker.

The publisher and author are grateful for permission to reprint the following copyright material:

Dannie Abse: extract from *Ash on a Young Man's Sleeve* (Robson Books, 2002), copyright © Dannie Abse 2002, reprinted by permission of the Chrysalis Group plc; **Air Cadets:** extract from leaflet 'Challenge yourself', reprinted by permission of www.aircadets.org; **Maya Angelou:** extract from *I Know Why the Caged Bird Sings* (Virago Press, 1998), copyright © Maya Angelou 1969, reprinted by permission of Time Warner Book Group UK; **WH Auden:** 'Refugee Blues' from *Collected Poems*, (Faber, 2007), reprinted by permission of Faber & Faber Ltd; **BBC news:** extract from article 'The world's most dangerous road' (www.bbc.co.uk, 11.11.2006), reprinted by permission of the BBC; **Alan Bennett:** extract from *The History Boys* (Faber, 2004), reprinted by permission of Faber & Faber Ltd; **James Berry:** 'Hurricane' from *The Hutchinson Book of Children's Poetry* edited by Alison Sage (Hutchinson, London 1998), reprinted by permission of The Peters Fraser and Dunlop Group Ltd; **Alan Bold:** 'Autumn' reprinted by permission of The Random House Group; **Harold Brighouse:** extract from *Hobson's Choice* (Samuel French Ltd, 1956), copyright © 1916 Harold Brighouse, reprinted by permission of Samuel French – London; **Bill Bryson:** extracts from *Notes from a Small Island* (Black Swan, 1996), reprinted by permission of the Random House Group Ltd; **Robert Cormier:** extract from *Heroes* (Puffin Books, 1999), copyright © Robert Cormier, 1998, reprinted by permission of the Penguin Group; **W H Davies:** 'Leisure', from *Songs of Joy and Others*, (Fifield, 1911), copyright © W H Davies 1911, reprinted by permission of Kieron Griffin as Trustee of the H M Davies Will Trust; **Shelagh Delaney:** extract from *A Taste of Honey* (Grove Press, 1994), copyright © 1956 by Theatre Workshop (Pioneer Theatres Ltd), reprinted by permission of Grove/ Atlantic Inc.; **Roddy Doyle:** extract from *Paddy Clarke Ha Ha Ha* (Minerva, 1994), copyright © Roddy Doyle 1993, reprinted by permission of Reed Consumer Books Ltd; **Carol Ann Duffy:** 'Havisham' and 'Valentine' from *Mean Time* (Anvil, 1993), reprinted by permission of Anvil Press Poetry; **Ruth Fainlight:** 'Handbag' from *Staying Alive: Real Poems for Unreal Times* edited by Neil Astley (Bloodaxe, 1995), reprinted by permission of Ruth Fainlight; **Stace Fielding:** article: 'Should girls be allowed in the Boy Scouts?', *Helium* (www.helium.com), copyright © 2002-2010 Helium, Inc. reprinted by permission of Stace Fielding; **William Golding:** extract from *Lord of the Flies* (Faber, 1954), reprinted by permission of Faber & Faber Ltd; **Tanni Grey-Thompson:** extract from 'Treat me as a person first' from http://www.tanni.co.uk, reprinted by permission of Tanni Grey-Thompson; **Tony Harrison:** 'Long Distance II' from *Tony Harrison Selected Poems* (Penguin, 1987), reprinted by permission of Penguin Books Ltd; **Seamus Heaney:** 'Follower' from *Open Ground: Poems 1966-1996*, (Faber, 1998), reprinted by permission of Faber & Faber Ltd; **High North Alliance:** extract from *Marine Hunters: Whaling and Sealing in the North Atlantic* (High North Alliance, 1997), reprinted by permission of High North Alliance; **Amelia Hill:** extract from 'How Jamie saved me' *The Observer* 22.12.2002, copyright © *The Observer* 2002, reprinted by permission of Guardian News and Media Limited; **Home Office:** extract from leaflet 'Steer clear of car crime', copyright © Crown Copyright; **Nick Hornby:** extract from *About a Boy* (Penguin, 2000), copyright © Nick Hornby 2000, reprinted by permission of Penguin Books Ltd; **Ted Hughes:** 'Hawk Roosting' from *Collected Poems*, (Faber, 2003), reprinted by permission of Faber & Faber Ltd; **Mecca Ibrahim:** extract from article 'Why we all hate Jamie Oliver' reprinted by permission of Peter Kenny, www.anothersun.co.uk; **Kazuo Ishiguro:** extract from *Never Let Me Go* (Faber, 2005), copyright © Kazuo Ishiguro 2005, reprinted by permission of Random House, Inc.; **Jenny Joseph:** 'Warning' from *Staying Alive: Real Poems for Unreal Times* edited by Neil Astley (Bloodaxe, 1995), reprinted by permission of John Johnson Ltd; **Charlotte Keatley:** extract from *My Mother Said I Never Should* (Methuen, 1988), copyright © Charlotte Keatley 1985, reprinted by permission of Methuen Drama, an imprint of A & C Black Publishers; **Harper Lee:** extract from *To Kill a Mockingbird* (Wm Heinemann 1960/Vintage 2004), copyright © Harper Lee, reprinted by permission of the Random House Group Ltd, and Aitken Alexander Associates; **Amanda Little:** extract from article 'Manchester City are making a mockery of the game', *News & Star* 28.10.2009, copyright © *News & Star* 2009, reprinted by permission of CN Group; **Llandudno Tourist Board:** extract from leaflet, reprinted by permission of Llandudno Tourist Board; **Louis MacNeice:** 'A Prayer Before Birth' from *Collected Poems 1966* (Faber, 2007), reprinted by permission of David Higham Associates Ltd; **Jack L. McSherry III:** extract from 'How to Survive a Bear Attack', www.arcticwebsite.com, reprinted by permission of Jack L. McSherry III; **Namibia Tourism Board:** extract from brochure 'Namibia: Land of Contrasts', reprinted by permission of the Namibia Tourism Board; **Alden Nowlan:** 'In Praise of the Great Bull Walrus' from *Between Tears and Laughter* (Bloodaxe, 2004), reprinted by permission of Bloodaxe Books; **Mary Oliver:** 'Morning' from *Wild Geese: Selected Poems* (Bloodaxe, 2004), reprinted by permission of Bloodaxe Books; **J B Priestley:** extract from *An Inspector Calls* (Heinemann Plays, 1992), copyright © J B Priestley 1947, 1992, reprinted by permission of PFD (www.pfd.co.uk) on behalf of The Estate of J B Priestley; **Rhondda Heritage Park:** extract from leaflet reprinted by permission of Rhondda Cynon Taff County Borough Council; **Willy Russell:** extract from *Blood Brothers* (Methuen, 1995), copyright © Willy Russell 1983, reprinted by permission of Methuen Drama, an imprint of A & C Black Publishers; **Save our Stanley:** extract from website http://saveourstanley.co.uk, reprinted by permission of Accrington Stanley Football Club; **Siegfried Sassoon:** 'Base Details' from *The War Poems* (Feather Trail Press, 2009), reprinted by permission of the estate of George Sassoon; **Owen Sheers:** extract from *Resistance* (Faber, 2007), copyright © Owen Sheers 2007, reprinted by permission of Random House, Inc.; **Rachel Shields:** article 'Glad to have been a Girl Guide', *The Independent*, 23.08.2009, copyright © 2009 Independent News and Media Limited; **Sports Council Wales:** extract from 'Health Challenge Wales' brochure www.sports-council-wales.org.uk; **John Steinbeck:** extract from *Of Mice and Men* (Penguin, 2006), copyright © John Steinbeck 1937, 1965, reprinted by permission of Penguin Books Ltd; **Allan Stratton:** extract from *Chanda's Secrets* (Annick Press, 2004), copyright © Allan Stratton 2004, reprinted by permission of Annick Press Ltd; **Meera Syal:** extract from *Anita and Me* (Flamingo, 1997), copyright © Meera Syal 1996, reprinted by permission of HarperCollins Publishers; **Dylan Thomas:** 'Do not go gentle into that good night' from *Dylan Thomas Selected Poems 1934-1952*, copyright © 1952, 1953 Dylan Thomas, copyright © 1937, 1955, 1956, 1957 by the Trustees for the Copyrights of Dylan Thomas, copyright © 1938, 1939, 1943, 1946, 2003 by New Directions Publishing Corporation, reprinted by permission of David Higham Associates Ltd/ New Directions Publishing Corporation; **Welsh Tourism Board:** extract from leaflet 'Get out and enjoy the big country', reprinted by permission of Welsh Tourism Board; **Amanda Whittington:** extract from *Be My Baby* (Nick Hern Books, 2005), copyright © 1997 Amanda Whittington, reprinted by permission of Nick Hern Books.

Although we have made every effort to trace and contact all copyright holders before publication this has not been possible in all cases. If notified, the publisher will rectify any errors or omissions at the earliest opportunity.

AO2 Studying Spoken Language

- Understand variations in spoken language, explaining why language changes in relation to contexts.
- Evaluate the impact of spoken language choices in their own and others' use.

Frequently asked questions

How long will I have to do the task?
You will write your final response in a two-hour Controlled Assessment in school or college. It could be split into parts, provided your teacher collects the work in at the end of each session. You will, of course, have a generous amount of time to do the research connected with the task before the event.

What are the rules relating to research and planning?
During the research and planning stage, you have to work under limited supervision. You can collaborate with other students in discussion groups and research activities, but you have to provide your own individual response for assessment. You may make use of research materials in the preparation period.

How much help can my teacher give me?
Your teacher can give you advice of a general kind, but is not allowed to give you a detailed writing frame, nor detailed help with drafting. Your final piece of writing must be produced under formal supervision.

What should my final study look like?
It is fair to say that it should look like an essay, with all the normal advice applying. A decent length might be three to five sides of file paper, assuming you have average-sized handwriting. To quote from the advice on writing literature essays: "Anything much less than three sides is likely to be not detailed enough. Anything longer than five sides may be long-winded – the best candidates are sharp and selective with their ideas."

How much is this assessment worth?
The spoken language study is worth 10% of the assessment in GCSE English Language.

How can I prepare for the Controlled Assessment?
You need a very basic outline structure, so that you know where you're heading. Think in terms of a structure that allows you to write two or three paragraphs a page for three to five pages.

How should I start to write my essay on the day?
Start with purpose. Address the question, and explain the main thrust of your essay, offering a brief trailer perhaps. Do not waste your first paragraph on a lengthy introduction.

EXAMINER'S TIP

- When writing your response, you will need to structure your paragraphs well in order to sustain your essay sensibly over a few pages of writing. As in a literature essay, it will also be very useful to quote on occasions and refer to other details to support the points you wish to make.

Acknowledgements

The publisher and author would like to thank the following for their permission to reproduce photographs and other copyright material:
p13: OUP; **p14t:** Serg64/Shutterstock; **p14m:** Herbert Kratky/Shutterstock; **p14b:** Pichugin Dmitry/Shutterstock; **p15:** Graham Bell/Photolibrary; **p16-17:** Gail Johnson/Shutterstock; **p18t:** Sinopix/Rex Features; **p18b:** Rolf Hicker Photography/Photolibrary; **p19:** Mark Whitfield/Rex Features; **p22:** Alex Livesey/Getty Images Sport/Getty Images; **p27:** Topical Press Agency/Hulton Archive/Getty Images; **p29:** Julian Makey/Rex Features; **p37:** Image100/OUP; **p39:** Milena Lachowicz/Shutterstock; **p40t:** David Berry/Shutterstock; **p40-41:** zhu difeng/Shutterstock; **p41t:** Tatiana Grozetskaya/Shutterstock; **p41b:** John Riley/epa/Corbis; **p42-43:** Andrei Rybachuk/Shutterstock; **p45:** Eric Gevaert/Shutterstock; **p46:** Morten Hilmer/Shutterstock; **p47:** Andreas Gradin/Shutterstock; **p48:** Sergey Kurnikov/Dreamstime; **p54-55:** Photodisc/OUP; **p56:** Carlos Arranz/Shutterstock; **p59:** Paul Popper/Popperfoto/Getty Images; **p61:** Rusty Elliott/Big Stock Photo; **p64:** Photodisc/OUP; **p67:** Trinity Mirror/Mirrorpix/Alamy; **p69:** Roberto Cerruti/Shutterstock; **p73:** Mikael Damkier/Shutterstock; **p75l:** Stringer/Getty Images; **p75m:** Sutton-Hibbert/Rex Features; **p75r:** The Art Archive/Alamy; **p77:** English School/The Bridgeman Art Library/Getty Images; **p80b:** Ronald Grant Archive; **p81t:** Donald Cooper/Photostage; **p81b:** Alastair Muir/Rex Features; **p90-91:** Corbis/OUP; **p93:** MGM/The Kobal Collection/Cooper, Andrew; **p94:** Reuters/Corbis; **p95:** c.Icon/Everett/Rex Features; **p100:** Tischenko Irina/Shutterstock; **p102:** Working Title/The Kobal Collection/Sparham; **p104:** Andrey Shadrin/Shutterstock; **p107:** Denis Vrublevski/Shutterstock; **p108:** Douglas Mccarthy/Mary Evans Picture Library; **p109:** Castle Rock/Columbia/The Kobal Collection; **p110:** Everett Collection/Rex Features; **p113:** Ronald Grant Archive; **p114:** Ronald Grant Archive; **p117:** Everett Collection/Rex Features; **p118:** Ronald Grant Archive; **p119:** Ronald Grant Archive; **p122:** Feng Yu/Shutterstock; **p124:** Karkas/Shutterstock; **p125:** Fox Searchlight/The Kobal Collection; **p126:** David Fisher/Rex Features; **p133:** M_ART/Shutterstock; **p134:** Manor Photography/Alamy; **p135:** Factoria singular fotografia/Shutterstock; **p136:** Photos 12/Alamy; **p137:** mehmetcan/Shutterstock; **p138:** Paul Banton/Shutterstock; **p139:** grynold/Shutterstock; **p141:** Robert Daly/Getty; **p142l:** Voronin76/Shutterstock; **p142r:** baki/Shutterstock; **p153:** Laurence Gough/Shutterstock; **p155t:** Photodisc/OUP; **p155b:** Mona Makela/Dreamstime; **p156t:** Clara/Shutterstock; **p156m:** Palabra/Shutterstock; **p156b:** Tetra Images/OUP; **p158:** Tetra Images/OUP; **p159:** Mav/Dreamstime; **p160l:** Anthony Charlton/AP Photo; **p160r:** Phil Walter/Getty Images Sport/Getty Images; **p161t:** Karel Gallas/Shutterstock; **p161m:** Eddie Keogh/Reuters; **p161b:** Ben Stansall/AFP; **p163:** Hartmut Schmidt/Photolibrary; **p164:** Ray Stubblebine/Reuters; **p167:** Zerra/Shutterstock; **p168t:** Rex Features; **p168b:** Christoph Weihs/Shutterstock; **p169:** Helmut Meyer Zur Capellen/Photolibrary; **p173:** Senai Aksoy/Shutterstock; **p177:** c./Shutterstock; **p178t:** Comstock/OUP; **p182b:** Monkey Business Images/Fotolia; **p180:** Adrian Sherratt/Alamy; **p183:** Rex Features; **p184:** Hinochika/Shutterstock; **p185:** Corbis/Digital Stock/OUP; **p186:** Karen Moskowitz/Getty Images; **p187:** Valueline/OUP; **p188:** Paul Doyle/Alamy; **p190:** Photodisc/OUP; **p191:** Pawel Libera/Photolibrary; **p192:** Yuri Arcurs/Shutterstock; **p194:** AL Accardo/Masterfile; **p195:** endostock/Fotolia; **p196:** John Penezic/Shutterstock; **p198:** Masterfile; **p199t:** Photodisc/OUP; **p199b:** VladKol/Shutterstock; **p200t:** Yuri Arcurs/Shutterstock; **p200m:** Design Pics/OUP; **p200b:** Comstock/OUP; **p202:** BananaStock/OUP; **p206:** Blend Images/OUP; **p207:** Yuri Arcurs/Shutterstock; **p209:** Jim Laws/Alamy.
Cover image: GlowImages/Alamy

Illustrations by Mark Brierley, Emmanuel Cerisier, Martin Sanders and Rory Walker.

The publisher and author are grateful for permission to reprint the following copyright material:

Dannie Abse: extract from *Ash on a Young Man's Sleeve* (Robson Books, 2002), copyright © Dannie Abse 2002, reprinted by permission of the Chrysalis Group plc; **Air Cadets:** extract from leaflet 'Challenge yourself', reprinted by permission of www.aircadets.org; **Maya Angelou:** extract from *I Know Why the Caged Bird Sings* (Virago Press, 1998), copyright © Maya Angelou 1969, reprinted by permission of Time Warner Book Group UK; **WH Auden:** 'Refugee Blues' from *Collected Poems*, (Faber, 2007), reprinted by permission of Faber & Faber Ltd; **BBC news:** extract from article 'The world's most dangerous road' (www.bbc.co.uk, 11.11.2006), reprinted by permission of the BBC; **Alan Bennett:** extract from *The History Boys* (Faber, 2004), reprinted by permission of Faber & Faber Ltd; **James Berry:** 'Hurricane' from *The Hutchinson Book of Children's Poetry* edited by Alison Sage (Hutchinson, London 1998), reprinted by permission of The Peters Fraser and Dunlop Group Ltd; **Alan Bold:** 'Autumn' reprinted by permission of The Random House Group; **Harold Brighouse:** extract from *Hobson's Choice* (Samuel French Ltd, 1956), copyright © 1916 Harold Brighouse, reprinted by permission of Samuel French – London; **Bill Bryson:** extracts from *Notes from a Small Island* (Black Swan, 1996), reprinted by permission of the Random House Group Ltd; **Robert Cormier:** extract from *Heroes* (Puffin Books, 1999), copyright © Robert Cormier, 1998, reprinted by permission of the Penguin Group; **W H Davies:** 'Leisure', from *Songs of Joy and Others*, (Fifield, 1911), copyright © W H Davies 1911, reprinted by permission of Kieron Griffin as Trustee of the H M Davies Will Trust; **Shelagh Delaney:** extract from *A Taste of Honey* (Grove Press, 1994), copyright © 1956 by Theatre Workshop (Pioneer Theatres Ltd), reprinted by permission of Grove/Atlantic Inc.; **Roddy Doyle:** extract from *Paddy Clarke Ha Ha Ha* (Minerva, 1994), copyright © Roddy Doyle 1993, reprinted by permission of Reed Consumer Books Ltd; **Carol Ann Duffy:** 'Havisham' and 'Valentine' from *Mean Time* (Anvil, 1993), reprinted by permission of Anvil Press Poetry; **Ruth Fainlight:** 'Handbag' from *Staying Alive: Real Poems for Unreal Times* edited by Neil Astley (Bloodaxe, 1995), reprinted by permission of Ruth Fainlight; **Stace Fielding:** article: 'Should girls be allowed in the Boy Scouts?', *Helium* (www.helium.com), copyright © 2002-2010 Helium, Inc. reprinted by permission of Stace Fielding; **William Golding:** extract from *Lord of the Flies* (Faber, 1954), reprinted by permission of Faber & Faber Ltd; **Tanni Grey-Thompson:** extract from 'Treat me as a person first' from http://www.tanni.co.uk, reprinted by permission of Tanni Grey-Thompson; **Tony Harrison:** 'Long Distance II' from *Tony Harrison Selected Poems* (Penguin, 1987), reprinted by permission of Penguin Books Ltd; **Seamus Heaney:** 'Follower' from *Open Ground: Poems 1966-1996*, (Faber, 1998), reprinted by permission of Faber & Faber Ltd; **High North Alliance:** extract from *Marine Hunters: Whaling and Sealing in the North Atlantic* (High North Alliance, 1997), reprinted by permission of High North Alliance; **Amelia Hill:** extract from 'How Jamie saved me' *The Observer* 22.12.2002, copyright © *The Observer* 2002, reprinted by permission of Guardian News and Media Limited; **Home Office:** extract from leaflet 'Steer clear of car crime', copyright © Crown Copyright; **Nick Hornby:** extract from *About a Boy* (Penguin, 2000), copyright © Nick Hornby 2000, reprinted by permission of Penguin Books Ltd; **Ted Hughes:** 'Hawk Roosting' from *Collected Poems*, (Faber, 2003), reprinted by permission of Faber & Faber Ltd; **Mecca Ibrahim:** extract from article 'Why we all hate Jamie Oliver' reprinted by permission of Peter Kenny, www.anothersun.co.uk; **Kazuo Ishiguro:** extract from *Never Let Me Go* (Faber, 2005), copyright © Kazuo Ishiguro 2005, reprinted by permission of Random House, Inc.; **Jenny Joseph:** 'Warning' from *Staying Alive: Real Poems for Unreal Times* edited by Neil Astley (Bloodaxe, 1995), reprinted by permission of John Johnson Ltd; **Charlotte Keatley:** extract from *My Mother Said I Never Should* (Methuen, 1988), copyright © Charlotte Keatley 1985, reprinted by permission of Methuen Drama, an imprint of A & C Black Publishers; **Harper Lee:** extract from *To Kill a Mockingbird* (Wm Heinemann 1960/Vintage 2004), copyright © Harper Lee, reprinted by permission of the Random House Group Ltd, and Aitken Alexander Associates; **Amanda Little:** extract from article 'Manchester City are making a mockery of the game', *News & Star* 28.10.2009, copyright © *News & Star* 2009, reprinted by permission of CN Group; **Llandudno Tourist Board:** extract from leaflet, reprinted by permission of Llandudno Tourist Board; **Louis MacNeice:** 'A Prayer Before Birth' from *Collected Poems 1966* (Faber, 2007), reprinted by permission of David Higham Associates Ltd; **Jack L. McSherry III:** extract from 'How to Survive a Bear Attack', www.arcticwebsite.com, reprinted by permission of Jack L. McSherry III; **Namibia Tourism Board:** extract from brochure 'Namibia: Land of Contrasts', reprinted by permission of the Namibia Tourism Board; **Alden Nowlan:** 'In Praise of the Great Bull Walrus' from *Between Tears and Laughter* (Bloodaxe, 2004), reprinted by permission of Bloodaxe Books; **Mary Oliver:** 'Morning' from *Wild Geese: Selected Poems* (Bloodaxe, 2004), reprinted by permission of Bloodaxe Books; **J B Priestley:** extract from *An Inspector Calls* (Heinemann Plays, 1992), copyright © J B Priestley 1947, 1992, reprinted by permission of PFD (www.pfd.co.uk) on behalf of The Estate of J B Priestley; **Rhondda Heritage Park:** extract from leaflet reprinted by permission of Rhondda Cynon Taff County Borough Council; **Willy Russell:** extract from *Blood Brothers* (Methuen, 1995), copyright © Willy Russell 1983, reprinted by permission of Methuen Drama, an imprint of A & C Black Publishers; **Save our Stanley:** extract from website http://saveourstanley.co.uk, reprinted by permission of Accrington Stanley Football Club; **Siegfried Sassoon:** 'Base Details' from *The War Poems* (Feather Trail Press, 2009), reprinted by permission of the estate of George Sassoon; **Owen Sheers:** extract from *Resistance* (Faber, 2007), copyright © Owen Sheers 2007, reprinted by permission of Random House, Inc.; **Rachel Shields:** article 'Glad to have been a Girl Guide', *The Independent*, 23.08.2009, copyright © 2009 Independent News and Media Limited; **Sports Council Wales:** extract from 'Health Challenge Wales' brochure www.sports-council-wales.org.uk; **John Steinbeck:** extract from *Of Mice and Men* (Penguin, 2006), copyright © John Steinbeck 1937, 1965, reprinted by permission of Penguin Books Ltd; **Allan Stratton:** extract from *Chanda's Secrets* (Annick Press, 2004), copyright © Allan Stratton 2004, reprinted by permission of Annick Press Ltd; **Meera Syal:** extract from *Anita and Me* (Flamingo, 1997), copyright © Meera Syal 1996, reprinted by permission of HarperCollins Publishers; **Dylan Thomas:** 'Do not go gentle into that good night' from *Dylan Thomas Selected Poems 1934-1952*, copyright © 1952, 1953 Dylan Thomas, copyright © 1937, 1955, 1956, 1957 by the Trustees for the Copyrights of Dylan Thomas, copyright © 1938, 1939, 1943, 1946, 2003 by New Directions Publishing Corporation, reprinted by permission of David Higham Associates Ltd/New Directions Publishing Corporation; **Welsh Tourism Board:** extract from leaflet 'Get out and enjoy the big country', reprinted by permission of Welsh Tourism Board; **Amanda Whittington:** extract from *Be My Baby* (Nick Hern Books, 2005), copyright © 1997 Amanda Whittington, reprinted by permission of Nick Hern Books.

Although we have made every effort to trace and contact all copyright holders before publication this has not been possible in all cases. If notified, the publisher will rectify any errors or omissions at the earliest opportunity.